I hope t. enjoy Kara

Cyberwink:

One woman's inside scoop on maneuvering the Web's "meet market."

KAREN RISSLING

Copyright © 2011 Karen Rissling

All rights reserved.

ISBN 978-0-9839006-0-3

DEDICATION

To my parents for showing me what a real and loving relationship looks like after 46 years.

ACKNOWLEDGMENTS

Mom And Dad: Thanks for your love and encouragement, which made me believe that I could finish what I had started. (And for all the blog subscribers you rustled up for me, Mom!)

Jennifer Mares: For your listening ear, shoulder to lean on, and constant encouragement...I am grateful. For your incredible copy editing skills and bleeding red pen, I am indebted!

Mike Givens: You've been so helpful in brainstorming cover ideas and book titles- not to mention your fantastic advice in the online dating tips section of this book!

José Loya: Thanks for helping give the women looking for love online some great counsel in the online tips section! Your quick wit and charm shone through. Maybe you should write a book?

Jessica Dekoning: Thanks for using your talents and creativity to help make this book cover look so appealing!

Ada Koppejan: Thanks for listening to all these stories over the years, and then helping me design the interior and cover of this book. You knew that left to my own devices, this book might have been published in 2015!

Ruben Aguirre: Thanks for designing a beautiful website (www.karenrissling.com) and giving me the family and friends discount. You are very talented!

My blog subscribers: I love writing posts for you! Your feedback is always sought after and appreciated!

And last but not least....

Barnes and Noble and Starbucks for providing me a safe place to meet these online suitors! Also thanks to the **Baristas** that would cheerfully make my coffee drinks during those long writing spurts... ☺

Who is Karen Rissling, and What Makes Her an Expert on Online Dating?

INTRODUCING MYSELF TO people I don't know is something that I am fairly used to doing. Since I was in school, I have always been the proverbial "social butterfly". Flitting from person to person, and getting chastised for talking during class (though the teachers still liked me), was a regular occurrence. For almost as long as I can remember, I have always been a raging extrovert. After graduating from university, I was fortunate enough to have the opportunity to do volunteer/missions work for well over a decade, which provided countless opportunities to meet new people.

That journey led me to encounter a variety of diverse individuals, as I globe-trotted and had the unusual privilege of serving the destitute and needy. The organization I worked with would host multiple camps in Juaréz, Mexico, before the drug cartels invaded and took control. Through these events, I would meet hundreds of people over spring break alone.

Little did I know when I began this endeavor that online dating would turn out to be similar to maneuvering in a cartel war zone, but the battle would now take place in coffee shops, restaurants, and other public venues. The ultimate conquest? To find a lasting love. Without getting pulverized.

Throughout my 20's I went from one serious relationship to another. I did not date. I was the type of girl that a guy seemed to want to marry, not just go to the movies and make out with. For me, this was a positive phenomenon, as I looked for long-term possibilities each time I went out with someone new. It was as though I emitted an invisible signal which declared that all players should keep walking, and that any serious contenders who were looking for a girlfriend, were welcome.

Three and a half years. A year and a half. A year and a half. Three and a half years. You add all of these relationships up and that is the decade where I always had someone who thought of me, who called me, and who sent me flowers, poetry, emails, care packages, letters (depending on the guy, of course), and I loved every minute of it. I am a relationship woman, which has made the next phase of my life an interesting one, to say the least.

About the time that I broke up with my serious boyfriend of three and a half years, I was rapidly approaching thirty. Now, unless a woman has already hunkered down and gotten married and had children, this milestone is a big deal. There is something devastating about saying goodbye to your twenties, where the world is still your oyster and time is still your friend.

You don't give a second thought to the responsibilities you carry in your "grown up" career, or what kind of anti-aging face cream to purchase while drifting through your twenties. In a culture where beauty is closely associated with youth, it can be daunting to say farewell to that assurance and that safety. Maybe thirty was not as catastrophic an age for me because I looked years younger than I actually was. I attribute that good fortune partially to genetics (You should see my mom!), and to clean living. Because of the fact that everyone thought I was in my twenties, I just thought of myself as having "lots of time" to meet the right guy. There was no rush. I still hear that I am a pretty girl. A supermodel, I definitely am not, but I have received my fair share of attention, and have often been labeled the "attractive girl next door" type. Surely, time had not run out for me to find love?

As mentioned previously, it was not unusual for me to meet new people, but the problem was that those new people tended not to be any single men my age. While still doing mission work, the staff members I'd come across were teenagers, couples, and families. Not many single guys in their late 20's or early 30's seemed to be focused on missions. When I transitioned into teaching at a public middle school, the pickings were even slimmer. The men were all older than me, married, or they were interns who were fresh-faced college students. One year I had a great intern, who bordered on "Enrique Iglesias" good looking. All my preteen girls were undeniably "in love" with Mr. Martinez! I also enjoyed checking out his shiny hair and straight teeth from afar in a "non-pervy", totally-legal, sort of way. Even though we'd play tennis for a few years after his year-long stint in my classroom, I could not bring myself to show interest in a boy who was *at least* 10 years my junior.

Having spent a good amount of time doing missions, it should be obvious that my faith is important to me. Thus, the question that has kept surfacing over the years is, "Surely you can meet an eligible bachelor at church, right Karen?" Wrong. In my whole post-twenties dating career, I have only met two men at church. One of those relationships ended so badly that I left a church that I had truly loved attending. It was too awkward to deal with the drama and the gossip that encircled that situation. The second man was a serious enough beau, who actually made the trek to meet my parents and spend Christmas with us in Canada, but in the end, it seemed that the timing was off. Add to this, the fact that I usually ended up joining all-women bible study groups, and it was unlikely that without extensive church-hopping, I would run into Mr. Right.

In our society, if a woman has never been married by the time she reaches her thirties, people start to sit up and take notice. There are only so many times that I can hear the following phrases from well-intentioned onlookers:

"It will happen when the time is right."

"The right guy will come along when you least expect it."

"I can't believe you have NEVER been married. You are so great!"

So now I have resigned myself to online dating. I have been doing it for over ten years, and I have gone on more dates than I can count, even while taking some extended breaks. I have had some absolutely unforgettable experiences; both terrible and exhilarating. What I do not have are any regrets. What I have ultimately gained is an "online romance" education.

A disgruntled suitor, who knew I was writing this book (and knew he would be included in it), accused me of cruelly mocking people through sharing these dating escapades. This could not be further from the truth! I have used humor to discuss why different dates did not lead to anything more, but I would never deliberately wound anyone or injure their egos out of spite. My own ego was hurt plenty of times, as you will see, when someone I liked was "just not that into me". I suspect my quest is one to which millions of women, and dare I say men, can relate. Match.com commercials boldly declare that 1 out of every 5 relationships now begins online, and due to how fast-paced and hectic our lives have become, I believe it. Even though seeking a mate (or even just a date) this way has become commonplace, many singles remain tight-lipped when it comes to admitting that they are willing participants in the online pursuit for love.

Not me. I am about to let the cat out of the bag.

Ten years.

Thousands of cyberwinks.

Countless dates.

Buckle up; this is going to be a bumpy ride.

Where it all Started

SURROUNDING ME WERE party-anticipating, tight-bodied coeds in their early twenties, giggling and obnoxiously spouting off phrases like, "I am going to get so wasted!" or "I can't wait to hit that." Never had I seen an airport so packed with enthusiastic revelers, eager to get to their hotel pool bar to taste their first watered down piña coladas. The heat generated from so many people made me feel slightly disoriented as I searched for my mom, who was due to beat me to Cancun by half an hour.

Little did I know that this trip would result in much more than me simply getting that perfect tan, or respite away from the rigid schedule that had become my life. Starting my first year teaching while still going to school had been what some would call a challenge, and nearly impossible for the faint hearted.

As if I was not busy enough, there was also my side business, which involved selling jewelry at home shows. After years of volunteer work, the profit margin of 50% was a great source for equipping my classroom with all the supplies that a first-year teacher needs. This endeavor, however, ate up a few Saturdays or Sundays a month - precious time that was needed for lesson planning and studying. My parents' motto often rang in my ears, "If it doesn't kill you, it will only make you stronger."

This is not to say that there hadn't been encouraging moments over the last couple of months. Surprisingly, I had been nominated for student teacher of the year for the University of Texas, El Paso, which I thought was amusing, as the observer had come to visit during one of my least exciting lessons. She had also chosen to evaluate me as I taught the class that all first-year teachers are "stuck with"; the one where most of the students have issues and behavior problems. Despite all the obstacles, the students and I had genuinely bonded, so professionally, I felt like I had found my niche. I was where I belonged.

My love life seemed to be the only area I could think of, that needed serious improvement. I had been asked countless times why I was not yet married, and I chalked it up to my jetting off to different countries doing volunteer missions work. All that traveling can really make a girl inaccessible, I supposed. This seemed to be the reason many attributed to my still single status, as I had been told that I have a warm, laid back personality, and that I am not that hard on the eyes.

As mentioned in my introduction, throughout my 20s I had been a serial dater, with one committed relationship after another. In fact, at 19, I had gotten engaged. Well, sort of. My older and very devoted boyfriend had bought me a diamond ring, presenting it to me on Christmas Eve. My startled and completely inappropriate response had been, "Is this a friendship ring?" His stare spoke of devastating disappointment at my reaction, and his reply was, "Let's just call it a promise ring for now."

All of those boyfriends had fallen along the wayside as I had struggled with a real fear of commitment. I had decided that although I had loved them, I wasn't in love with them. There was one exception - the case of the one man I had truly fallen for, who had smashed my heart into smithereens.

A good friend of mine had met (ironically, online) and married, an air force man in Florida. While stationed there, she and her husband had run into Mike, one of his colleagues, at the gym on base. After learning more, she convinced him that he absolutely needed to get to know me, and a long distance courtship ensued. I had never experienced such a strong emotional connection with a man before, and was keen to see what could develop.

Just when we were about to seriously consider how to make a relationship work between us; he received his orders to be stationed in the Netherlands for three years. As far as I knew, from what he had told me, he'd never slept with anyone before he left the U.S. Due to some difficult times that befell him in Europe, and some impulsive decision making, he ended up getting a girl pregnant; ruining what, I had felt at the time, was a perfect future together. I still remember getting a phone message from him less than a week before he was to return to the States:

"Hi Karen, This is Mike. Livingsworth. I wish you were there because I really want to talk with you. I am being stationed about 4 hours from your house in Albuquerque, New Mexico. I have really missed you and want to talk with you so much! I love you and I am excited to be moving so close so we will be able to spend so much time together again. Won't that be wonderful? I wonder if you are seeing someone or if you are still available? I cannot wait to hang out with you again. I will call you in the next day or two."

After two days of waiting with bated breath by the phone, I realized that something had gone dreadfully wrong. Later, I was to find out that the girl Mike had slept with in Poland had become pregnant, and he, being the stand up guy he was, had decided to marry her. She had called and told him the dismal news before he had a chance to speak to me, and after he had left that last phone message. Mike ended up with a bride he barely knew, while she ended up with her one way ticket to America, the Promised Land.

I don't know if I have ever completely recovered from the loss of that relationship. Maybe subconsciously I have held all of the other guys who have come along my path, up to the ideal of Mike. Reading this you may wonder what was so great about him, especially after how everything turned out. All I can say was that there was that inexplicable, dare I say soul-mate type chemistry, which only materializes every once in a great while. Although he had a hero complex, and had been "snowed" by a woman with a hard luck story, he was also kind, funny, and genuine. After the door slammed shut on this relationship, it was time for me to move on.

Being a very outgoing type of girl, I have done my share of dating since, deciding that if within 3 months I was not feeling a long-term vibe, it was better to cut the relationship off. While I've had fun meeting people, I have to admit that there have also been times when I would rather have been home in my pajamas watching Law and Order SVU with a bowl of popcorn and a Diet Coke, than going out on another first date. Sometimes the whole dating scene just didn't seem worth the effort! Add to the mix that the guys I had been conversing with online tended to be long distance, and I would go through the process of getting to know them, only to discover, once we met, that the chemistry or the timing was off.

Right before this trip with my mom to Mexican paradise, I had been tirelessly scoping out the electrical technicians who were hired to work on our newly-renovated school. None of the other teachers were even remote possibilities for dating, and my friendly conversations with an attractive tech named Roger had been thrilling until my friend Susan subtly, ok not so subtly, asked him if he had a girlfriend. Of course Susan didn't pose these personal questions in my presence, so that he wouldn't know that I was the one potentially interested. Good old Roger had been married for 11 years with several kids, which he neglected to mention during any of the 20 million hallway conversations we had shared (Oh yeah, and while you are at it, you may want to put on a wedding ring, Casanova!).

Once I found out the truth, I even brought up the subjects of marriage and children to see if Roger would come clean, yet he continued to shamelessly flirt with me, unwilling to admit he was a man with a family of his own! It was a day to celebrate when all the electrical work in our school was completed, and Roger was permanently out the door. I think it was soon after this point where I finally resolved to meet someone locally by going online. I had dabbled with it briefly in the past, with limited success.

This was how I had met Jason, an adorable military guy I would otherwise never have met. Late night talks in his car, gently holding hands at the movie theater during our first flick, I felt that this could possibly be a relationship that was going places. Being that he was the first guy that I had dated locally in eons, I was definitely hopeful; even optimistic. Wow! This guy has some real promise, I had thought.

Things almost seemed too easy with Jason. He called when he said he would, and even sometimes when he hadn't promised to. Helping me look over some of the papers I had to grade, there was never a complaint about how I couldn't just be carefree and go to the movies at the drop of a hat. The compliments were many, and looking deeply into his bright green eyes, I would forget about my "to do" lists and responsibilities for the moment. You probably thought from this description that we went out for months, but actually this relationship was rather short-lived.

One night after sushi and a movie, Jason and I had driven to a manmade lake in a nearby neighborhood. The moon was out, the stars were sparkling, and we got out of the car to walk a little. It was just as romantic a moment as I had ever read described in any novel. As we strolled, fingers entwined, Jason stopped under a tall tree. Tenderly he pulled me in for our first kiss. I had been very impressed with how much of a gentleman he had been up to this point. As the kiss took a more urgent turn, Jason whispered into my ear.

"What was that babe?" I asked not able to make out what he was saying.

"Let's go back to your place." he hoarsely muttered.

Now I am not the type of girl to do this after knowing a guy for a couple of weeks. Correction. I am not that type of girl at all! I had assumed this fact had been made clear, as we had discussed beliefs about morals and our relationships with God. Yet, here was my "gentleman" not acting too gentlemanly.

Needless to say, when Jason dropped me off at home, he suddenly had decided that his upcoming trip to Korea, where he was to be stationed, would be too hard on our budding relationship. I believe his cheesy line went something like this: "I would rather hurt now than miss you later." Part of me wanted to scream, "So about 15 minutes ago you were ready to sleep with me and then hightail it for Korea?!" The more dignified Karen said goodbye, and as she waved, knew that she would never hear from Mr. Green Eyes again.

Being shoved by a halter-top-wearing blonde in painted on capris, I was rudely jolted from my memories back into reality. I was in Mexico, in the airport. The combined smell of sweat and cheap perfume assaulted my senses as I started to wonder again why my mom and I had picked Cancun as a peaceful retreat during Spring Break. After about an hour of jostling people and trying to decipher the many incoming flights from Canada, I finally spotted my mom at one of the baggage carousels, and as quickly as humanly possible, we grabbed our rolling bags and took a taxi to our hotel.

The resort where we stayed in Playa Del Carmen was secluded and practically removed from the complete party atmosphere that reigns in Cancun during that time of year! In fact, there were not many people at all, which was what we had desperately hoped for - peace and quiet! Watching the lapping waves, with magazines and books in hand, I felt peaceful. Serene even. Spending time with my mom was novel as I don't get a chance to see her that often, with her living in Canada and my home being in Texas. The moment that would stand out for years occurred after showering, while getting ready for dinner on the second night of our stay.

My Mom cleared her throat and mentioned that she wanted to show me something. By her rigid movements and the intensity of her gaze, I could tell that what she wanted to discuss was deceptively important, despite her breezy tone. Bracing myself, I matched her casual timbre, "Sure Mom, what's on your mind?" Reaching into her purse for a piece of paper, she handed me what looked like a magazine article. Normally the types of articles my mom carefully trims and saves for me have to do with good eating and exercise practices, so I immediately suspected that she thought I was looking a little too hefty and needed to relay this information pronto.

I braced myself to feel slightly offended, and was already preparing my "they were in the dryer too long" defense argument for why my jeans were fitting so snugly. Very much to my surprise, my mom sheepishly addressed me while handing over the article, "Karen, it seems like you are just not meeting a lot of quality Christian men - maybe this information could help you." Sitting on the bed, eyes glued to the clipping, I realized that this article was about the World Wide Web, specifically the World Wide Web of DATING.

Now for those of you who have never had the pleasure of knowing my mother, she is not exactly what you would call a risk taker. The fact that she was actually encouraging me to go out and meet completely unknown males was a little daunting. What about "stranger danger" mom? Despite her love for security and safety, my mom had found an article for me about internet dating, purposely highlighting a Christian dating site.

"I can't believe that I have finally found my soul mate, and now we will be together forever!" raved one testimonial.

"I never knew there was such a great girl out there for me!" gushed a subscriber.

"We are getting married in a month!" claimed another.

As my eyes glanced over all this information, I couldn't pinpoint whether my emotional response should be to feel insulted by the overt cheesiness of these claims, or to be open to what I was reading, and the possibility that this could be a valid venue for meeting potential suitors.

During the next five days, I started to wonder if possibly posting a profile on a Christian website, or any website, could be helpful. After all, there could be a variety of different men at my fingertips. Even with Jason, one of my first local online interests, (whose story I just told), I had momentarily enjoyed what had seemed to be success - he had been cute, funny, and driven. The downside of my time with Jason was that he knew he was cute and funny, and he was clearly driven by the desire to get me into bed as quickly as possible, with no intention of commitment!

Terrible dates, cat calls, and clumsy hit-on attempts. I had endured more of these than I thought I could stand in the last few years in the black hole of attempting to date in El Paso. These less than satisfying experiences pushed, even rudely shoved me, to strongly consider if online dating was going to provide opportunities for me to meet guys with whom I could be compatible. It sure beat wondering if a stranger would approach me in a grocery store to ask me if a melon was ripe, or use some other equally lame pick up line. And let's face it, even those are usually few and far between - I didn't foresee a strapping, handsome, young man knocking on my front door asking for directions.

I was tired of going to church, sitting alone, and seeing the happy couples and families together. If I had to be subjected to watching any more backs being caressed or loving secrets being whispered into each other's ears, I felt I was going to vomit. I was tired of going to weddings or baby showers, and having innocent strangers ask me if I was married or had a boyfriend. I was tired of fielding the complimentary but painful statement/question, "I cannot believe that a woman like you is not married yet! How is that possible?"

It came to mind, as maybe it has occurred to you or to your unattached friends, that perhaps I would need to be more proactive in helping love happen in my life. Not being a "bar star" (a girl who frequents bars on the prowl for men), or a clubber, it was time to broaden my horizons. Ironically, having my mom give me her "stamp of approval" to look online, served to launch me into this decade-long internet dating marathon. I want to share my experiences: the good, the bad, and the ugly, in the hopes that other singles out there will belly laugh, be encouraged, and not feel so isolated and alone, while they attempt to find that "special someone" in cyberspace.

They All Fall Down

These are the chronicles of those men who plummeted from potential.

THE FOLLOWING TALES are meant to be entertaining snapshots of scenarios that I experienced when maneuvering the Web's "meet market". Names have been changed to protect the identities of these men, as to not cause them any unnecessary humiliation or discomfort. I have recreated these scenarios as accurately as my hazy memory allowed. In some of the situations where I embarrassed myself or used poor judgment, I wish I could have changed my name to protect my own identity, but that is the price of putting yourself out there - all pride must be set aside! I'm sure many men and women who are currently dating online have similar, if not more traumatizing yarns they could share. In the quest for online love there were bound to be obstacles and landmines. Here are some of mine. These are the chronicles of those men who plummeted from potential.

.... ;-)

Mr. Brought My Baby On the First Date

> ... the child was the only bright beacon, proving that innocence and purity still existed, despite what the complete idiot sitting across the booth from me was trying to disprove.

When people read this title, I am sure that they are going to think that bringing a baby on a first date was the worst part about this online suitor. Let me tell you that this was not the case at all. In fact, the child was the only bright beacon, proving that innocence and purity still existed, despite what the complete idiot sitting across the booth from me was trying to disprove.

Mr. BMB, (to be honest I have forgotten his name, perhaps blocked it from my memory) started our lunch off with an apology that he had to bring his baby with him on the date. There were reasons, and I am sure that they were legitimate, but there is something a little peculiar about sitting in a booth with two guys, and only one of them possesses the ability to speak.

After suspending my disbelief at the chain of events, I internally decided that I should be diplomatic and give this man a chance. After all, he even had a respectable job as a lawyer. Not being particularly physically attracted to Mr. BMB, this was difficult. I really should have accepted this as the first sign that things were only going to get worse.

Once he had settled his little boy in a high chair, this gentleman proceeded to look me straight in the eye and ask, "You are pretty, and seem to be intelligent, and normal. Why are you not married yet?" To this day, I am not sure if he was interrogating or complimenting me. As a single woman, how do you even go about answering that question? Very strange. I gave him the standard reply about not having met the guy I wanted to spend my life with and not wanting to settle.

We continued on with some small talk that was less than stimulating, until he brought up the fact that I had done missions. First, he commented that as a missionary, I probably took "a lot of naps".

"What is that supposed to mean?" I thought to myself, "Is this dim wit telling me he thinks that only lazy people get caught up in volunteer work?"

In the next breath, he started to relay what I thought was going to be a sweet little story about how when he was in his early 20's he had volunteered to be a counselor at a Christian camp. What I was about to hear was surreal.

He went on to tell me that they would lead activities all day with the kids, pray and minister to them, but when the sun went down and the campers went to sleep, they would all smoke weed and have sex with each other. Eyes wide, a startled expression on my face, I was something that I rarely am - Speechless! Even this clueless oaf caught on that I was not impressed with the recollection of his less than stellar experiences as a "spiritual mentor" for kids. His reaction was one that I never saw coming, "Oh don't worry. I never smoked up!" Still stunned and silent, all I could contemplate was how after all the marshmallows had been roasted, and the campfire songs had been sung, he had done the dirty with who knows how many of the counselors there! After about 1½ hours of verbal torture and a mediocre meal, I managed to escape. The verdict was in, and this lawyer was not an eligible man for me!

.... ;-)

Up in the Air Carlos: is He Gay or Straight?

I noticed he bounced when he walked, with a type of strut you just don't see straight men utilize. No, no, no. He is just a cheerful individual, not confined to the constraints of society's view of how a man should saunter.

I started flirting with this handsome guy on Match.com because he seemed like a very sweet person. He was an artist, yet worked a very manly occupation where he fixed mechanical problems with airplanes. As it turned out, when I contacted him, Carlos was heading out on a road trip to visit his family, and was about to pass right through El Paso. It seemed effortless for us to meet up, so we decided to do just that.

I remember this event as though it just happened. I was heading to the restaurant, excited to meet this man who seemed really down-to-earth and genuine. It was a high stress time in my life - I had just quit my very first teaching position in one district, and was to start training for a new teaching position in a different district. It was my birthday weekend, and so I thought it would be great to meet this "new guy", as he represented new possibilities.

As I entered the restaurant, I saw him, and my first thought was, "He is absolutely adorable." He is half Hispanic and half Caucasian. It is not uncommon for me to fall for biracial men, because they tend to be unusually attractive. His eyes were sparkly and his smile was fun-loving. Immediately, we had no problems relating or finding things about which we could easily talk.

After an enjoyable dinner, Carlos invited me to come out to see some of his artwork in his car. I was curious, and so he took some out of the trunk to show me. I was raving about it, since I can't even draw stick figures or rainbows. Don't we all admire someone who can create something that we can't?

Then, as we sat there, he suddenly turned and kissed me. It was very cute, and completely unexpected. He was only staying in town that one night, so he invited me to his hotel room to watch TV with him. I felt that we had talked enough, and that I would be safe with him there. He was not a large, muscular guy, and to be honest, I thought I could have taken him in a fight if it had come down to that.

Once we were in his room, we hung out, watched some non-descript TV, and continued our "canoodling" from the car. Strangely enough, Carlos did not try anything physical with me besides kissing. You may be thinking, "Come on, it was a first date, he shouldn't try anything else!" Anyone who knows me is aware that I am not a "loose woman", but let me plead my case, and present the evidence. In front of Carlos was a girl who he had already kissed, and he was now cuddling with, while watching a show on television in a hotel room. Most guys would at least try to get away with a little bit physically, even knowing they are not going to get far. His lack of forwardness was very unusual, but I wrote it off to him being tired after a long road trip. Also, when I got up to leave, he actually allowed me to walk out to the car by myself! Certainly not very chivalrous of him.

Even though we did get along well, there was no discussion as to the next time we would hang out. After all, it wasn't like he lived on the other side of town; he lived in another state!

Off and on I would hear from Carlos via random texts, phone calls, and emails. Then, a few years later he called out of the blue to tell me he would be back in town, and asked if I wanted to go and see a movie with him. Remembering his dimples and dark brown eyes, I figured that it was no big deal to hang out with him again. However, I had no idea if this was to be considered a date, or simply a friendly reunion. Either way, it was a night out, and I just wanted to enjoy some male company!

We decided to meet at Barnes and Noble for coffee, and then head over to watch a movie. At first glance, when I ran into him at the magazine kiosk, "Is Carlos gay?" immediately ran through my mind. I racked my brain trying to recall details from our first date a few years before. Had there been any tell-tale signs that should have tipped me off to his sexual preference? At this point, Carlos went in for a hug, which also felt ambiguously friendly, with just a hint of interest, due to its length.

Just how long should a hug between acquaintances last anyway? Had he ever spoken about any past relationships with women? I couldn't remember. Admittedly, nodding as I listened to him describe his road trip, he did appear to have more feminine mannerisms than I had remembered. Subtly looking him up and down, a few key things caught my attention. His jeans were unusually tight for a man, and he was wearing a low v-neck t-shirt with a couple of different necklaces. His hair was perfectly coiffed, and his shoes modern and stylish. Some of you are questioning me, believing that Carlos might fit under the label of "metrosexual". This inkling did occur to me, and I decided to entertain it as a possibility. This was before the years of the TV show "Jersey Shore", or I would have thought he was emulating one of the male cast members.

We strolled over to the adjoining café for a latte. Sitting across from this delightfully energetic hunk, I found myself silently excusing little idiosyncrasies that appeared a little "off" for a straight guy. Had he been flirting with my favorite barista, who was opening dating men? No, no, no. Carlos was just being friendly, and was nice to everyone! I noticed he bounced when he walked, with a type of strut you just don't see straight men utilize. No, no, no. He is just a cheerful individual, not confined to the constraints of society's view of how a man should saunter. In fact the freedom of his stride was amazing, considering that his pants were as tight as mine after a good buffet meal!

During our chat in the café, I did try to dig into his personal life somewhat, but with limited success. I only heard a story about one person who I believe was named Pat, or perhaps Chris, who could just as easily have been a man as a woman. Unfortunately, the recollection provided no distinguishing details to confirm his or her gender. I think there may have been a Sam as well. Apparently, I would be receiving no answers this evening.

Defeated, I surrendered my escalating curiosity to my wish to see the flick we had previously planned to watch.

In line at the theater, Carlos was standing quite close to me. As Murphy's Law would dictate, one of my middle school students spotted us, came over to say hi, and winked at me mischievously. I knew for sure that this would get around to his classmates, as they were always, and inexplicably, fascinated with my romantic life.

No arm finagled its way over the back of my seat, and no leg subtly brushed up against mine. In fact no "move" of any kind was made in the movie theater. Once we were alone again after the show, Carlos was still being chatty and charming. I just couldn't seem to shake the fact that I almost felt like I was out with one of my girlfriends. A couple of times throughout the evening I had also noticed that when Carlos would answer his cell phone or check a text, it was usually from another guy. After he had checked one message, he practically squealed, "OMG, that guy is crazy!"

It is only left to be said that after the movie we parted ways, as he had to get an early start in the morning, and to be honest, I just couldn't take the ambiguity any longer. If I spent that much time out with a man wondering about his orientation, would he be the right fit for me romantically? Could I date a man who was prettier than me, and who probably spent more time getting ready for the evening than I did? As it turned out, Carlos and I have remained friends, and I still have no idea whether he likes men or women. Although he had spoken about flying to visit me, it just never worked out, which was probably for the best.

All of us women need a Carlos, right? Just not as a boyfriend!

.... ;-)

The Nice Guy, Nice Time, Nice Knowing ya

Even though you will not remember the names of these suitors 24 hours later, try not to think of these dates as a waste of time, but as a means to an end.

Nothing bad happened - nothing dramatic ensued, decent enough conversation, possibly peppered with a few awkward silences. This is the nice guy you know you will never see again. These types of dates can even go on for several hours.

More than once, I have been with gentlemen at great restaurants, where we have had decent two-way conversations for an extended time. These men were polite, courteous, and pleasant to be around. As non-threatening as this may sound, does it sound like a recipe for romance to you? If you are seeking a mate online, you will likely go on a parade of dates like this. Don't lose heart. Don't resign yourself to a life of comfort eating and adopting cats from shelters.

You may start to wonder if you are being too picky. Let me assure you, you aren't. Keep your head up and keep answering those incoming emails from prospective men. One day you will meet one who will make your heart pound and your palms sweat. I believe it is a numbers game. For every man I have met with whom I felt a real connection, there were probably ten nice guys with whom I sat through dinner or coffee.

Don't become discouraged, and remember that going on a date with a nice guy who is not right for you, is better than being involved with any of the guys you may encounter who suffer from undiagnosed mental disorders or might treat you badly. Even though you will not remember the names of these suitors 24 hours later, try not to think of these dates as a waste of time, but as a means to an end. As long as you were amiable and treated the person with respect, then chalk it up to experience, and make plans for your next rendezvous.

.... ;=)

Aaron: the Ageist

He countered with little witty comments about driving Miss Daisy, and how he was in diapers when I was already in legwarmers.

One night, while perusing profiles, I received an instant message from a decent looking, dark haired guy in the 26-30 years old category. (All sites have age categories into which their members are confined) He told me about how he really enjoyed reading my profile, and said he would like to chat. It is vital to mention the age groupings in order for this tale to make sense. I learned the hard way that to divulge my real age, (37 at the time), was an open invitation for guys over the age of 50 to tell me how they had houses and cars, but no pretty young things to share them with.

Before I sound like an ageist snob, this would be the right time to interject that I have nothing against older men, but I was a young 37, not ready to morph into someone's sofa sidekick. I've got a lot of living to do, and a sense of adventure that doesn't quit. I don't want to talk about a man's grandchildren when I have not yet even had a child of my own.

Back to my story. So this young buck and I are chatting and hitting it off - LOL at each other's jokes, and ROTFL (rolling on the floor laughing - for the texting/instant messaging amateurs out there ☺). Near the end of the conversation, I tell him how old I am. He is only 27. Although I feel a slight twinge of disappointment at that, I tell myself that I should remain open.

Maturity differs radically depending on the individual man. Aaron could've been the epitome of maturity for all I knew.

Also, there was nothing riveting on TV, so I mused, why not roll the dice and chat with him? He admitted that he was a bit shocked that I was 37, but said he wanted to talk on the phone, since he felt we had such a strong connection while instant messaging. Now, I had put myself in the 31-35 age category, so really I was only 2 years off of what the maximum was for this age group. We teased each other a bit, with me telling him that before we could talk on the phone, he would need to fax me a permission slip signed by his parents. He countered with little witty comments about driving Miss Daisy, and how he was in diapers when I was already in legwarmers.

The next day we took our internet relationship to new heights and spoke on the phone. It was an engrossing, fun conversation, with enough sprinkles and dashes of serious topics for me to see that this guy might have potential. Intelligence? Check. Witty and humorous? Check. Sensitive yet manly? Check. Personal and authentic relationship with God? Check.

Aaron suggested the following day that we talk on land lines so that we wouldn't be so frequently interrupted by our cell phones' dropped calls. After another 3 hour long conversation, I got off the phone a little shell shocked, but generally content. (He was talking about going off to do missions with far away tribes, and inquired if that would be something I would be open to in the future). Maybe the 10 year age difference was not a big deal after all? Maybe I could sacrifice Barnes and Noble to work with tribeswomen in the town of #*#*$&#(@^@^@yaba, where I would likely be required to dig my own latrine, pluck my own eyebrows, forgo my occasional froufrou latte at Starbucks, and never watch another fluffy reality TV show again!

All day at school, I had a little extra bounce in my step. At the end of the previous night's conversation, Aaron had asked me to call him the next night if I had an opportunity. During my prep time, I graded all my students' essays with the speed of a veteran racecar rushing toward the finish line. I didn't want to worry about having to finish work when I might be occupied by another lengthy conversation with Mr. Maybe.

After a quick gym workout, I went home and performed my daily hotmail check. There I saw an email from Aaron. Awwwwwww. How cute - he couldn't wait to send me a little note to tell me how he thought about me today. In the subject line were three little words, "A few thoughts…" Let me see if I can more or less recreate his condescending email:

```
Karen I have been reflecting a lot since our phone
conversation last night. You are such a quality person and
have so much to offer to someone.
```

Any woman, or even man, reading this right now thinks that there is a proverbial "but" that fits in right here. It is the buttering up before the bomb drops. Maybe not. Can't a guy just give a girl a compliment?

Ok, you thought right. There was TNT looming in the background.

```
BUT as I have been thinking all day about things, I have
concluded that the age difference may be a factor, and with
time that will grow. I know you will make someone a great
wife, and I will greatly miss our conversations.
```

Are you kidding me? Mr. Chimmychanga future missionary to foreign tribesmen was giving up a smart, funny, and dare I say, attractive girl, because I was too OLD?

Quickly and efficiently I composed a reply to dear Aaron, wishing him the best in his search and telling him how great it was to meet him.

Yeah right! Did I not tell this little sniveling punk how old I was while we were still only instant messaging on the computer? I was not the one wanting to talk each day. I fired off a feisty, slightly confrontational (but not desperate sounding), note letting him know that if he wanted a *girl*, he needed to browse the 21-25 category. I wished him luck finding a *girl* that would go to Chimmychanga land with him, and who actually possessed the intellect, wit, and the maturity he was seeking. The tone was not friendly, but what was he expecting, when he dismissed me solely on the fact that I had lived longer than he had?

.... ;-)

The Perverts

When you get an email from a complete stranger, asking you for topless pictures, you are going to be tempted to throw in the towel.

Okay my female cohorts looking for love, I am about to state the obvious, even though it would seem that all of you would know that this is bound to be one of the major pitfalls of attempting to find your dream man on the Internet.

When you get an email from a complete stranger, asking you for topless pictures, you are going to be tempted to throw in the towel. Either that, or you are going to feel so dirty, that you'll want a towel to use after attempting to scour yourself clean to remove that filthy word film from your brain.

Some guys are overt in what they are looking for in a woman, and will make sure to state their demands in their profiles. Some websites even house specific sections where people can obviously, and dare I say proudly, state that they are looking for hook-ups without strings. "Intimate Encounters" and "Casual Dating" are a few examples of these.

If you frequent these areas of the sites, prepare yourself, because the perverts are rampant, and they are assuming that you are just as pervy as they are!

There are also men frequenting these online hot-spots who are garden variety "just want to get into your pants" types; so if you are looking for a long-term commitment, limit your searches on dating sites to men who clearly state they are looking for relationships.

Other "gentlemen", and I use the word loosely, will be perverts who are disguising themselves as love seekers. There will be phrases used in their profiles such as:

- **I know that my soul mate is out there, and will search until I find her.** Translation: I will sleep with as many people as I possibly can until I find "her".
- **I am just an honest, generous guy looking for an honest girl.** Translation: I going to use the word honest as much as possible, so you believe I actually have good intentions toward you.
- **Wanting to find that special person to cuddle on the couch with.** Translation: I only want to be on the couch with you if our clothes are discarded on the floor.

And one of my all-time favorites,

- **Enjoys long walks on the beach at sunset.** Translation: I want to get you to a nude beach before the sun goes down.

A guy friend told me once that men often use sentiments that they feel will touch a woman's heart deeply in order to gain her trust. Ever since, I've taken this advice to heart, as I read potential soul-mate profiles.

I am naturally leery of men who claim to be honest. Who is actually going to admit that he is a dishonest, self-seeking jerk? With grandiose, romantic declarations, these types of men may try to manipulate women's feelings in order to get what they want. There have been a few incidents in which these "perverts in hiding" have attempted to lure me in with their smooth talk, and then, attempted to get me to "talk dirty" to them. Some have expressed interest in various other types of activities, often involving web cams and slow removal of clothing. Clearly, if I had wanted to be a 1-900 number operator or a stripper, I would have chosen such a career path, or at least they would have been suggested by my high school guidance counselor.

Please note that if you are looking for a long-term, committed relationship, these men will not provide that for you.

.... ;-)

Gustavo: the Romantic Two Timer

Gustavo and I laughed, we kissed, we flirted, we kissed, we talked about our hopes and dreams, we ate in cute little cafes, we kissed.

Gustavo was one of the first guys I ever communicated with online. Ironically, I'd met this online Casanova on a chat site where I was attempting to practice my newly acquired Spanish, rather than trying to meet men. It was quickly apparent that in these chat rooms, the girls had no interest in talking to me, but that all the men did, and go figure, they all wanted to see pictures. At this point, I had emerged from a long-term relationship and was not trying to jump into anything new.

While all the guys seemed eager to help the Canadian "gringa" carry on with her limited and grammatically shameful Spanish conversations, there was one particular caballero who didn't appear to want the dialogue to go to that pervy place where you get asked what you are wearing...

After several online chats, we ended up talking on the phone, and because Gustavo was bilingual, we would speak in both languages. Talking about everything under the sun, it seemed that our personalities just clicked in that way that so rarely happens. You can only chalk that connection up to fate!

Months passed, and I was planning an excursion to visit my close friend, Katie, in Boston. Since Gustavo lived in New York, it seemed logical to figure out a way that we could meet in person and transform our online friendship into a real-life one.

Wandering alone around the streets of the Big Apple to have an encounter with an attractive Dominican man may seem risky to many, but my judgment of people's character combined with my sense of spontaneity were victorious. Off I went. The master plan was to take a train from Boston to New York, where Gustavo would pick me up. He had already arranged where I was going to stay, and looking back now, I realize that I foolishly trusted a stranger to take care of me in an unfamiliar place. In no way do I recommend that any women out there try this. It was reckless. Back then I did not have a working cell phone, and when I missed the train and had no way to contact Gustavo with the time difference in picking me up, I almost broke into a cold sweat!

Fortunately for me, as I exited the train and headed into the crowded, noisy terminal, he was there, waiting for me. Standing over six feet tall, with broad shoulders, muscular arms, and grinning at me from ear to ear, Gustavo seemed absolutely thrilled that I had arrived. This was the first time I had ever met someone in person that I had talked to online, and I had no idea what to expect. Would our super-charged connection be there in person like it was on the phone? What if we didn't get along and my few days in New York would be filled with awkward and uncomfortable chitchat where both of us would be wishing that time would fly to relieve us of the anguish?

Fortunately, quite the opposite occurred. The chemistry between us crackled like a well-tended to fire. It was as if we could not take our eyes off each other, and, if anything, conversation flowed as though we had been friends for years.

There are unclear memories of a taxi ride. I'm sure I must have looked out the window and taken in the sights, but I could not recount anything I had seen. Gustavo and I were completely consumed with each other. It was fascinating to put the voice together with the person, to observe his gestures and mannerisms. As we drove to drop off my bag at the hotel, the air around us was electric. Uproarious laughter and flirty glances were constant and spoke of the obvious interest present. It was only a matter of time before we kissed.

For the next few days, I existed in a romantic bubble, where reality could not forge its way in. Comedy clubs at midnight. Roaming down the busy streets of New York, we took everything in: horns beeping, the smell of car exhaust, all of the rushed professional people dressed smartly in black, and the world famous Times Square. My eyes were drinking in the scene before me, but were still parched. Gustavo and I laughed, we kissed, we flirted, we kissed, we talked about our hopes and dreams, we ate in cute little cafes, we kissed. We did not sleep together, but we did a LOT of kissing.

When the time came where I needed to hop a train back to Boston, there was heaviness in my heart. When would we see each other again? Even though it was obvious to me that Gustavo cared about me, was attracted to me, and we had somewhat of a soul-mate type connection, he was cryptic when it came time to talk about a potential future meeting. At the time, I did not understand why he was acting this way. I just blamed the distance and the drastically different places in which our lives were heading. I returned to Boston and then home, and prepared to accept that it was what it was, simply an impossible situation.

As you will read below, we continued to maintain semi-regular contact with each other via email and phone. I managed to salvage and include a few of these emails to show you that even though a man's heart may be longing for you, that does not automatically ensure that you are guaranteed to be granted possession of it. Although I was not aware that Gustavo had a girlfriend, it wasn't an unrealistic conclusion to which I could've jumped. We were not officially together, and a caring guy like him should've been with someone, even if it was not with me. The question was not officially asked; therefore I was able to avoid an answer I did not want to hear.

As stated previously, after that first trip into New York, Gustavo and I did keep in touch. That spark had not gone out. Around the time I was due for another visit to see my friend Katie in Boston, Gustavo generously offered to make the trip out to come and hang out with us.

From the moment we picked him up from the train station, it was as if we had never been apart. The fun that was had! Katie and her husband, and Gustavo and I, lived it up for the few days we were all together!

Strolling through downtown Boston, hitting the comedy club, going out on the town dancing; it was as though the stars were shining just a little bit brighter each night. To enjoy myself more would not have been possible, until I suddenly caught Gustavo in a lie. What happened was that at the end of the evening, before his impending departure the next morning, he had needed to take an important call. I could tell this was not just a friend calling to shoot the breeze. Not meaning to, I overheard him telling his girlfriend (so he did have one!) about why he had needed to come out to Boston on "business".

Abruptly, I was confronted by the fact that I was the other woman, and it was repulsive! Karen Rissling is NOT the other woman! I'm the wholesome girl next door, who never even looks at another woman's boyfriend or husband. All of the old feelings we had shared had already come racing back between us, and Gustavo confessed that not only did he have a girlfriend, but he lived with her. I remember feeling a sharp pain, and my throat started to ache. My eyes began to water. "I will not cry," I remember thinking to myself. Then I did. Gracefully though, not where you sob and your nose starts running, like those women on "The Bachelor" who failed to receive a rose. Don't be fooled, though, the damage was extensive.

As the explanation for his actions surfaced, I listened in disbelief. According to Gustavo, he was in love with two women. His live-in girlfriend was Dominican and a part of his culture and past. I was someone he had met and never expected to fall in love with, especially with the distance and circumstances that created insurmountable complications. There was no denying he felt a soul mate connection with me. This was a lose-lose situation, and we both knew it:

> Hi Karen:
> I read your e-mail and I couldn't help feeling really sad. I wished I could have been there with you so we could help each other deal with this ordeal. First of all I want to keep in touch with you as much as I can. I wouldn't want to lose your friendship for nothing in this world because it is part of my most precious feelings.
>
> K, I'm as convinced as you are that timing had a great deal to do with our special attachment not being able to blossom. When I first saw you I knew I was bound for a conflict with my heart. I just didn't expect yours to be broken in the process as well. I hoped our friendship had meant a lot to both of us, but I thought it would not reach the level it did. I won't say what I could have or should have done for this dream to work out. I know now that although we won't be together I will never be able to forget about you and everything that you mean to me. G

Even though it sounds ridiculous, I believe that Gustavo was between a rock and a hard place. As you can see from his email, (and there were numerous others that I did not include) he treasured our friendship, and it wasn't like I was sleeping with him, so that was not his ulterior motive. He genuinely felt that he cherished two women and was lost as to what to do about it. I, personally, have never been in love with two people at once, so it is difficult for me to relate, but I don't believe that he had intentionally set out to hurt me. I believe the following emails where he expressed his feelings were genuine:

> How are you K? I have been doing a lot of thinking about our last conversation Monday morning. Knowing you, you'll probably tell me not to worry about anything and that everything is forgiven, but still a sour taste remains in my mouth after everything that was said. I didn't know whether to email you or not because I have already caused you too much pain and disappointment. I never intended it to be that way, and I swear the last thing I expected to happen was for me to use you. Now that I have heard you say I had used you let me ask you the following:
>
> -Why would I have traveled such distance to do such a terrible thing?
>
> -Why, all of a sudden, did I want to forget about everything that has happened between us and just be a perfect Jerk?
>
> My explanation for both of these must be that since I first met you I decided that the perfect ending for my drama game (you always tell me that I am the king of drama..) was to come visit you at a perfect location near NYC to break your heart. I think this is the first time when our views of something are as opposite as South from North.
>
> I wanted to learn and I was helped to learn. I couldn't help falling for her. I couldn't help seeing I was almost breaking three hearts. That's when I thought that maybe I could save all three hearts by not being selfish and wanting to have it all. I know that I could make the person who would love me forever happy. I just didn't know I was going to fall for two people. I hope you don't think this whole thing is silly or anything.

```
I thought that maybe the best thing that could have happened
was for me to have not come to see you in Boston. We could
have saved each other the awkward situation we are in right
now. We would have stayed just the best friends we were
before all this happened and believe me I wish I could go
back in time to do just that because the one thing that
causes me the greatest pain I have ever experienced is
causing pain to anyone else, even more to those I care so
much for.

Sorry about everything, always here,

G.
```

The lesson I learned from this Dominican beau was that sometimes you need to ask the tough questions, even if you don't want to hear or accept the answers to them. Gustavo and I are not in contact anymore, but I still have a picture of us showcased in my apartment. Forgiveness reigns, and above all, he was a treasured friend to me, despite our unusual situation.

Author's Update: Recently Gustavo and I did come into contact with each other, although correspondence is minimal. The reason for this is that he is married now, and his wife is the girlfriend he was with when I knew him. They are expecting their second child, and I am happy for them.

.... ;-)

Justin: the Reason to Use Caution

Maybe my Saturday nights from now on would be filled with flirty and fun dates with this handsome stranger who would become my boyfriend, and then... my husband ... Wait a minute. Slow down Rissling. Don't buy the Bride magazine just yet!

If you skipped ahead to the online tips section of this book, you would recall how I mentioned that no matter how normal a guy appears during the first meeting, you should never get into a car with him as the date progresses. Meet Justin, who became the reason why this is a rule that I now follow religiously. Justin was someone who I actually did not meet online, but who approached me in the local Barnes and Noble bookstore. For those of you who have never been to this haven of free magazines and great coffee drinks, it is a place where I am a regular. Kind of like the bar "Cheers", where all the baristas there know my name.

One January day, I was journaling on my computer, which is something I usually commit to do continuously throughout the year (That lasts for about a month before my busy life intervenes and reflection takes a backseat to immediate demands).

Clueless about anything happening around me, I was typing away when I was approached by Justin. I heard a deep male voice confidently say, "Excuse me." Glancing up, expecting to be asked if someone was sitting at the next table occupied only by an empty plate, I caught a glimpse of an attractive, preppy man. He was clean cut, with short, dark brown hair and piercing blue eyes. This is my favorite physical combination in a man.

I quickly recovered from looking like a deaf mute by replying, "Hi." Even completely caught off guard, I managed to smile at him!

At this point, my preference was to meet some local guys. Instead of a long time investment of writing back and forth and lengthy chats online, I was impatient to meet someone to see if there was any kind of immediate personality connection and attraction present for both of us. I had experienced too many dead end internet "connections" lately. Besides, how did I know if these online guys were even who they said they were? I was obviously happy that there was a live, attractive man right in front of me!

Justin then asked me if it would be ok for him to sit down. Now I was wondering if I was part of some survey for his university psychology project. With a dazzling, boyish smile, he proceeded to tell me that he had seen me at Barnes before, that he had wanted to come over and talk to me, but hadn't had the nerve to do so. Because it was a new year, he had decided that it was time to take some risks, and one of those was to come and introduce himself. I felt very flattered! After all, this eye-catching guy had actually taken the initiative to talk to me, which is something that most men won't do unless they have had a dose of "liquid courage" at the local watering hole. At Barnes, the closest equivalent is a triple shot of espresso, and I didn't see a coffee cup in his hand.

With a partly conscious hair flip, I invited Justin to sit down. He quickly accepted and gallantly offered to buy me a drink. Over caramel light frappuccinos, conversation seemed almost effortless. I didn't have to worry about attracting Justin; after all he had sought me out. I didn't worry about impressing him, as I figured that if he got a feel for who I was, then he would like the real me, and things could progress from there. Justin had been in the military (air force) for the last 5 years, had traveled extensively, and spoke passionately of the love that he had for friends and family.

Of course, it did not take long for the conversation to move in the direction of what everyone who meets me wants to know. How in the world did a woman from Chilliwack, British Columbia (about an hour and fifteen minutes outside of Vancouver) end up in the border city of El Paso, Texas? Now, when men hear that I have done missions work, there are various types of reactions.

One of those is the impression that it will take a long time before they can charm me into bed. This is usually enough information for them to politely excuse themselves, and move on.

The second response is that they see me as being almost heroic, off on my business of saving the world! I do not find that flattering or favorable, because the problem with being up high on a pedestal, is that the fall is painful. The type of man that has this reaction also likes the fact that I do not appear to be a gold digger, since it isn't like missionaries are making the big bucks or living to obtain that brand new Coach purse! (No offense to those of you that like a nice handbag)

Another reaction I have come across is that they take it in stride as your life experience, and continue to get to know you. One strategy I had in introducing the fact that I was in missions, was that I would often bring it up casually, by telling young men that I did "volunteer" work. Then I would let them pace how much they actually wanted to know about the subject. With Justin, I just decided to hit him with the missions bullet straight on and see if he could take it.

When the question came up, as it always does, my answer was simply, "I am in missions." I expected to see a Justin-shaped, cartoon-like figure busted through the wall, in exit, but instead he calmly asked me the name of the organization. Did I detect a hint of healthy interest? As I explained the general idea, he burst out saying, "I am a Christian too." At this point, I was looking for that bright light to appear behind his head, and hear angels singing "Ahhhhhhhhhhhhh" in harmony!

After we continued to chat for awhile, I felt that it would be alright to meet him for dinner at Applebee's that Friday night. Public place. Lots of people would likely be there celebrating the end of yet another long work week, while watching the latest teams battle it out on the numerous TVs scattered throughout the room. It was just so refreshing to have a handsome guy actually make a bold move, that I decided the risk was worth it, and as mentioned above, it was a calculated risk. I would meet him there, so he wouldn't pick me up at home. My mom would have been very proud of my use of caution.

So as the day of reckoning arrived, I got ready with an undeniable feeling of growing optimism. There was definitely a spring in my step. Maybe this was meant to be. Maybe our run in was fate and God wanted us to be together. Maybe my Saturday nights from now on would be filled with flirty and fun dates with this handsome stranger who would become my boyfriend, and then… my husband …. Wait a minute. Slow down Rissling. Don't buy the Bride magazine just yet!

Sure enough, Justin was on time and waiting for me when I arrived at the restaurant. He gallantly opened the door and led me in, as we grinned foolishly at each other the way that you do on a first date with promise. Over the meal we talked about family and past history. Conversation flowed with ease, and as he leaned towards me, blue eyes sparkling, hanging on my every word, I felt like possibly one of the most interesting and beautiful women in the universe.

Being that it was a Friday night, it was obvious after we had hoarded our table for over 2 hours that the waitress was becoming frustrated. No more offers for drink refills. Constant glances to see if our payment was ready. Understandable. We needed to clear out so that the frazzled waitress could wait on other customers to earn tips for textbooks! It was the time on the date when it must be decided whether we took it to the next level, which was leaving the protection and the security of the restaurant. When Justin asked if I wanted to go and see a movie, I decided that would be ok, and this is where my attraction and "devil may care" attitude led me astray. I decided to ride with him and not take my own vehicle. Wrong decision.

At first everything was fine. We had decided to go to a movie theater across town to see a show that was not playing anywhere closer. As we continued to chat, suddenly the conversation took an unexpected turn.

"Can I ask you something?" Justin inquired.

"Sure. Shoot." I answered casually.

"Do you believe in aliens?"

"Whoa - wait a minute!" I thought, "This is a joke. I should laugh right?"

But his facial expression was not showing any hint that he was playing around with me. After a moment's hesitation, I simply answered, "Well, I have no reason to believe in them. Do you?"

Without any hesitation Justin responded, "Oh definitely! In fact, I feel that there are many life forms in space, and that we cannot assume that we are the only beings out there. That would be very egocentric."

"Did he just call me egocentric?" I thought to myself. I changed the subject to what I thought would be less controversial and less bizarre. "Justin, you were telling me how you are a Christian. Have you found a church that you like in El Paso?"

Still staring at the open highway ahead of him, Justin answered me, "I don't actually believe in organized religion. In fact I wouldn't mind going ahead and starting my own religion." My heart sank. At this point I knew we were not on the same wavelength about faith and beliefs. Without this in common, I knew we were doomed. I also decided that if he offered me Kool-Aid I was NOT going to drink it.

Then I realized.

My cell phone. "At least I have my cell phone," I thought. Unfortunately I only had one bar left. Why had I failed to charge my phone that afternoon? Then I remembered my battery had been burned out chatting to every person I knew that day, about this date with a handsome stranger I had met at the local book store. After all, up until the bizarre alien comment, this outing had all the elements needed to craft a romantic comedy plot. Now it was developing into a storyline, more suitable for a slapstick comedy (the joke is on me) or a science fiction flick! I couldn't think of a good enough reason to get out of seeing the movie by this point, and was much too polite to simply tell him that he creeped me out and that I wanted to leave.

Why do we, as women, have to be so agreeable? We don't want to hurt someone's feelings, but we put ourselves in jeopardy by being timid. Looking back at this "younger me" in this particular situation, I want to scream at her, "Get OUT of there! It doesn't matter if he feels slighted, or if he doesn't understand why you left! He is potentially crazy, and you are allowing yourself to be in a dark theater, and then in a car alone afterward with this psycho! Get OUT!"

Walking into the movie theater, we sat down and immediately Justin started making his moves on me. Being that he was an attractive guy, I was sure that he was used to girls who welcomed his advances. Just to be fair, there was no way for him to know that he had lost me at "alien".

About fifteen minutes in, Justin's seemingly innocent arm and leg "brushes" evolved into him putting his arm around me. Then he kept on turning my head towards his, touching my nose and saying, "What a cute nose you have." So not only was Justin acting oddly, but he was potentially blind too. I have my dad's nose, complete with a distinctive bump, and it is anything but "cute".

Tell me that I have beautiful eyes and I might believe you, as I have had many men praise that feature. He kept trying to grasp my hand, but I would maneuver it away to pretend to scratch that very cute nose I have, or my chin, arm, or other appendage. I was one step away from having to tell a boldface lie, and say I was having an allergic reaction to the popcorn. Unable to even enjoy the movie in the midst of all the groping, I just wanted to leave. Of course, the movie we had chosen, <u>Catch me if you Can</u>, was closer to 3 hours than to the typical 90 minutes.

As the credits finally started to roll, I sighed with relief. This was a mistake, as I believe that Justin took this sound as being a very deliberate sign of contentment, and was under the misconception that I'd really been enjoying this date.

As we made our way to his car, he familiarly put his arm around my waist, as though we had been a couple for months. Before opening the car door for me, Justin gave me a huge hug. Not sure what to do, I just patted his shoulder and subtly untangled myself.

"You are shy aren't you?" he asked as he settled himself into the seat, adjusting his rearview mirror.

"Shy?" I asked, "Really? You think so?" Where was he going with this?

"I think that you are one of those types of girls who would never cheat on her boyfriend. You are one of the last original good girls," he replied as he pulled onto the interstate.

"Well, I believe in having only one boyfriend at a time," I answered as I looked out at the miles and miles of dark, desolate desert. What is it they say? A desert is a great place to dump a body?

"You would never cheat on me like those other whores would!" proclaimed Justin, his eyes becoming dark and ominous.

"Am I in a horror flick right now?" I wondered, a little panicked. What was going on? Staying quiet for a few minutes, Justin seemed to be deep in thought. "Just make it back to your own car," I thought.

Then just as menacing as he had seemed moments before, Justin then proceeded to affectionately place his hand on my lower thigh, just below where my appropriate-length animal print skirt ended. Not feeling comfortable with this advance, I delicately took his hand and moved it from my thigh to his own. Looking into my eyes adoringly, he whispered something that I was not sure that I had heard correctly, "I am so glad that we are in a relationship now."

SCREEEEEECH!!!!! Slam the breaks on here! What was happening? Hadn't we been in each other's company for a mere 6 hours? I closed my eyes for a moment and then opened them again. Nope, Justin was still there, sitting beside me in this deceptively comfortable and normal car. This was not a bad dream - it was reality.

The next 20 minutes dragged its feet. "Act normally," I kept telling myself. Checking my cell phone, and seeing the battery's blinking red light, I felt it was mocking me for the foolish mistake I had made. Watching the pavement whiz by, I prayed under my breath that this wacko would take me directly back to my car, where I could make my great escape! As it turned out, my pleadings were heard.

When we returned to the Applebee's where this date had begun, I practically leapt out of Justin's vehicle. Quickly and in a monotone voice, I explained that we differed greatly in beliefs and ideologies, and that I did not see myself in a romantic relationship with him. At this moment, I was grateful to see various people scattered throughout the parking lot. They could serve as witnesses if anything dire went down, I silently speculated.

Justin's eyes widened and a look of disbelief and great irritation reigned on his features. "I CANNOT JUST BE FRIENDS WITH YOU... I AM ATTRACTED TO YOU, SO THAT WOULD BE IMPOSSIBLE!" At this loud outburst, an elderly couple turned around and looked at us with concern.

"Well, ok then. Thanks for a lovely evening!" Even before the words had all made their grand exit, I was practically sprinting to my car, which would soon be my haven and refuge from all the crazy that had been spewed continuously on me for what had felt like an eternity.

Breathing heavily, locking every door, and watching for any chance that this disturbed individual might tail me, I headed for home.

The moral of this tale is that if you do not know someone well, do not entrust your well-being to them. If your gut is telling you that you need to remove yourself from a situation, let's just say that your intuition is likely warning you of potential danger.

Looking back, I could have done so many things differently: excused myself during the movie and asked a friend to come and pick me up; feigned illness shortly after the alien comment came up before we had ventured too far from my car, and of course - not accepted a ride with a stranger! Knowing that this story could have turned out very tragically, I hope it will move you to lessen the risks you choose to take. Also, stop feeling so responsible for being polite on a date that feels wrong or sinister in some way. Find a way to extract yourself from the situation, and know that you have nothing for which to apologize!

.... ;-)

Short Fuse: the Ranter and Raver

Run, don't walk away from that kind of fury!

This tale is short and sweet, but is critical knowledge for the single girl who is looking for love. An attractive man, close to my age, from El Paso wrote to me, and seemed like a very sweet and complimentary guy. However, when I did not immediately respond to his email, he sent me a lengthy 5-paragraph email accusing me of playing mind games with him. He stated that he had previously thought that I was a good person, but had obviously been wrong. He went on to blast every part of my character; even proclaiming that I shouldn't even have been on the website, due to the fact that he had realized that I was not seriously trying to pursue a relationship with anyone.

I showed this to my friend, Ada, whose response was simply, "You need to block him."

My other pal's comment was, "Run, don't walk away from that kind of fury!"

Ladies out there, what you need to know is to beware of guys who come on strong at first, with lines such as "I never thought I would find a girl like you", when they have not had prolonged, or possibly any, contact with you.

What appears to happen is that such a man comes to the conclusion that you might be his dream girl, but the moment you accidentally, and innocently, shatter that illusion by doing or saying something that "disappoints" him, he becomes very volatile. This has happened to me a few times, and the best suggestion I can make is to block this type of man from any further contact. Do not be mistakenly flattered by his "passion" toward you, as this guy has serious issues with which one does not want to be saddled. There are legitimate reasons why this man is still single.

.... ;-)

The Military Wrestler With Ties to the Italian Mafia

Even though I was a young 39 year old at the time, even I know that Clinton and Stacey, (my makeover heroes on TLC's What Not To Wear) would not approve of a cherry red leather miniskirt and white thigh reaching boots on someone in my age group...or anyone of any age group.

Every once in awhile online, there will be a combination of crazy that no one else will ever encounter in the same way. I see Wayne as fitting snuggly into this category. I am not expecting anyone reading this to encounter an exact replica of "Wayne", but somehow the story still has to be told. Surely, each one of you brave online warriors will stumble across a variant of this type of individual, and you will wonder if you are the only person that has these kind of surreal run-ins.

Wayne wrote to me from one of the free websites on which I had been fishing for eligible men. Immediately, I felt that familiar tinge of "cougar"ness when I saw that his age started with the number 2, rather than with a 3, or now even with a 4! This was one of the last guys that I met before my personal online journey took a very different turn! He asked for my phone number to start texting me right away, and being that I was a bit bored, I threw caution to the wind and agreed.

Now, the first thing that I noticed about Wayne's texting style is that he usually only answered every question with one word. It is extremely difficult to get a read on someone like that! When I asked him what he enjoyed doing in his free time, he mentioned wrestling. Now, I have nothing against wrestling, it is a rigorous athletic activity that requires skill, agility, and according to Wayne, a girl in a short mini skirt and thigh high boots to blow colored powder into the ring at the beginning of a tournament! The kicker was that he wanted ME to do the honors of this "opening ceremony" for the insane during one of his fights!

I must own up to the fact that I have never actually watched any kind of wrestling live or on TV, so this could be a legitimate request that he was making. Even though I was a young 39 year old at the time, even I know that Clinton and Stacey, (my makeover heroes on TLC's "What Not To Wear") would not approve of a cherry red leather miniskirt and white thigh-reaching boots on someone in my age group … or anyone of any age group.

At first, when he mentioned this demand, I thought he was being funny. It was a good thing we were not engaged in a conversation, but texting, because I did let out a rambunctious laugh. I politely declined this invitation, but I still believe that he felt there was a chance that eventually I would give in and cave. Fat chance.

Right there I should have cut it off. Wayne was appearing to be a little off the wall, and I just was not getting that easygoing, casual vibe from him. In fact, he started calling me "babe". This is always a bit of a warning, because it means that this stranger is appearing to become emotionally attached to you; someone he doesn't know.

My friend Michael has always warned me that I am a beacon, a magnet for guys who are intense, clingy, crazy, and have issues. "You are too nice Karen!" he has declared on more than one occasion, "Losers and mentally unstable men gravitate to you, because you are nurturing and caring, and won't reject them outright." Even though I have been working on this "flaw" for years, I am still compassionate, even to my own detriment.

So I allowed Wayne to call me, thinking that there could be a chance that this was just one idiosyncrasy that could be overpowered by a charismatic personality, and some old fashioned values. A girl can dream right? When I agreed to the conversation, there was a small, and I admit, opportunist part of me that thought this could get a little peculiar, which could provide me with fodder for this book. The nicer side of me was thinking that this military transplant may simply be lonely and misunderstood.

No sooner had we said our hellos, than Wayne started campaigning for me to be his "ringside" gal. Using my selective hearing, while expertly changing the subject, I did manage to steer the banter in a different and much more sensible direction. However, I was sadly mistaken to believe that this route would be a normal one.

The topic of family is one that usually is safe and non-controversial when speaking on the phone for the first time. It is also telling as to how the man feels about his mom, dad, and siblings. Was family a priority for him? Did he have a good relationship with his mother? Was his upbringing one that would have laden him with emotional baggage?

Nothing could prepare me for the direction to which this discussion would veer next. As Wayne started to share about his childhood and relationships with his parents, it came up almost instantly that his Italian family had "connections". When I inquired what type of connections these might be, he replied very matter of factly that they were mob connections. Was this really happening? Was I talking to a guy, who if he was furious enough with me, could order a hit at the drop of a hat?

Oh, stop being so dramatic, Karen! I know that is what you are possibly thinking, but when this spawn of mobsters mentioned that his dad had gotten divorced and the "family" offered to "take care of it", I don't think I am making an unreasonable jump to reaching that conclusion. As luck would have it, I was just about to leave to visit my family in Canada for the summer, shortly after this first conversation. I was able to manage dodging his texts until I made a run for the border.

.... ;-)

Josh MD: Best First Date That Went Nowhere

My eyes drank him in like a big glass of ice water on a scorching hot day. Never in my wildest dreams was I expecting to meet a guy who was so incredibly good looking!

Meeting Josh was a risk that I was not usually willing to take. First of all, he wrote to me from, and expected me to respond to, a profile that had no pictures posted. Normally, in a case like this, I would automatically delete the message, because no profile picture usually is a VERY clear sign that this man has a face that only a mother could love. Don't judge me for being superficial! This is common practice in the online dating world! With great fear and trepidation, I decided to meet him at a local coffee shop. I chose this particular place because I almost never went there, and so if the meeting went awry, I wouldn't have to worry about ever setting foot into that place again. Are you overwhelmed by the sense of optimism I was feeling?

Anyone who has had the courage to meet a blind date, without the luxury of seeing at least one photo first, will sympathize with the blatant nervousness that plagues you just as you enter the door of the arranged meeting place.

Do I look ok?

How will I know who he is?

I don't want to just go up to any guy, in case it isn't him....

In my particular case, Josh had seen pictures of me on my profile, but I had not seen pictures of him.

The first reason with which he supplied me for not having photos posted was that he worked for the Sheriff's office and did not feel comfortable displaying his image on such a public forum. Secondly, he said that he did not have recent pictures that were uploaded to his computer. Normally, I would have run for the hills, but for some reason, I decided to take a chance and see what would happen.

When I called my best guy friend to tell him about the new escapade on which I was embarking, I was not encouraged. When I mentioned that this new guy would know what I looked like, but I would not know him, Ruben inquired, "What if you are not his type and he just sits there and pretends he is NOT the guy you are supposed to meet?"

As I gasped, he then added, "Or he might just look in the window, see you, and just stand you up." Although Ruben was kidding, he opened the door to my insecurity. It quickly crept in and grabbed me in a choke-hold. With friends like Ruben, I don't need enemies - I need a therapist.

Even when I am extremely nervous, I still have this pressing need to be on time, so I decided to go ahead, and like ripping off a band aid, just strutted into the designated meeting place, with my head held high. The small, obscure coffee shop was completely empty, or so it seemed. There were a few different sections, and finally I spotted a spiky hair cut belonging to a guy sitting in a big, red, comfy chair with his back to me. This just seemed so "movieish". You know - the part where the hero walks up to the bad guy, who then, on cue, suddenly spins his chair around to reveal himself!

Tentatively, I walked up, and the clicking of my high heel boots must have alerted him to the fact that I was approaching. He rose from his seat and turned around...

Suddenly I found myself blinded by one of the most dazzling smiles that I had ever seen. My eyes drank him in like a big glass of ice water on a scorching hot day. Never in my wildest dreams was I expecting to meet a guy who was so incredibly good looking!

After noticing the grin, my eyes traveled up to his piercing greenish-hazel eyes. There is nothing like a beautifully tanned Latino man with light-colored eyes (I had to consciously make sure I was still breathing)!

My gaze rested on his muscular chest and arms, but nothing prepared me for what would come next! My brain instantly computed that Josh had to be at least 6 foot 2. I LOVE tall men, and this was almost too much to handle without the time to process! Immediately, Josh grabbed me, enveloped me in an affectionate hug, and told me how great it was to meet me.

I don't remember if I responded in anything that would have resembled sensible English, but I must have, because he held out a chair for me, and we sat down. Within minutes he commented enthusiastically, "Wow, you are even prettier than your pictures!"

Seriously? I knew that I was wearing my lucky black shirt, but still!

Ok, when I state that I am wearing a lucky article of clothing, I know there are many women out there who can relate to this idea. You know that dress that always gets you that elusive second date? Or that shimmery blouse that often leads to that first kiss? Or even those pants that cause you to march into a job interview exuding unshakeable confidence?

Alright! We're back to the scene with the surprisingly gorgeous sheriff. The whole experience was starting to feel surreal. His admiring remark made me feel warm and fuzzy! He could not have thought of a better way to get me to relax and start attempting to charm him with my outgoing personality. Now that he had complimented my appearance, I felt that there was at least a chance of romance brewing. I was definitely feeling it!

After chatting for awhile, we decided that we would head over to the Northeast side of town to see a movie, since the one we wanted to watch was only playing there. Josh bought our tickets, and we went for coffee at Village Inn as we had time to kill before the movie was to start.

The conversation was entertaining. Tantalizing. Stimulating. We bantered back and forth, laughing and joking one moment, and then talking about serious topics the next. We both mentioned how there was a definite feeling that we had known each other for years! We even talked about our strong faith in God and our future dreams. (He was an aspiring doctor!) Was this all really happening on a first date?

During the movie, it felt like an electric current was flowing between us. I kept trying to subliminally send him the thought to make physical contact. You may laugh, but you know you have done this; willed the date you are with to make that first move.

Josh didn't hold my hand, but sat really close to me, murmuring little comments about the action on the screen. The movie plot itself was a blur, but I had never enjoyed a film more. In fact, I was ready to sit through a double feature if it had been permitted. I kept thinking to myself, "This is not happening! How could this perfect guy enter my life in such an unexpected way?"

Sauntering to his car after the film, we were still kidding around and teasing each other. At one point, I believe Josh even told me that we could have been brother and sister, separated at birth, since we were so similar in so many ways.

Looking back now, I should have viewed this comment as ominous foreshadowing. On the way home, it was obvious that this very late show, combined with the fact he had been working overtime hours all week, resulted in Josh being exhausted.

The movie theater was more than a hop, skip, and a jump away, and it would take at least 30 minutes to get back to my car that was still parked at the coffee shop where we initially met. From there, he still had to drive an additional 30 minutes home, and he had to get up before 6am the next day!

I offered to take the wheel while en route. He was so tired that he actually pulled over on the access road, and we got out to switch seats.

As I made my way toward his side of the car, Josh suddenly grabbed me! He started hugging me, and before it could have been predicted, he kissed me. This was not just a peck on the lips, but a full-blown passionate kiss. Kind of shocked, I responded enthusiastically - but not TOO enthusiastically (you girls know that fine line).

Long story short, he did fall asleep on the way to my car, and once we arrived at the coffee shop, I expected he would just hug me goodbye and head home.

The theme of this night should have been "astonish Karen", because this sleepy, Latin cutie then started making out with me in the car! Outrageous! After an undistinguishable amount of time, we finally said our goodnights. Sure that this would be the beginning of a promising relationship, I went to bed hugging my pillow like a giddy schoolgirl getting a note from her crush.

It did not take long to find out that reconnecting with Josh would be a disheartening task. In fact, it appeared that between his sheriff's department job, his daughter (he was a single dad), and his courses (biology, pre-med), he was extraordinarily busy!

As the days continued to pass since our fantastic first date, the fact that Josh was not calling or emailing me regularly was causing me to question if the whole experience had even happened, or at least had happened the way that I had envisioned it. Every once in awhile I would see him online and chat with him, until one night, weeks after our date, I called him out on how he had kissed me and led me on. His answer was that he felt that we had moved too fast, and it was causing him to lust.

WHAT? All we did was kiss, and even that was not uncontrollable! It sounded to me like a class-A-cop-out!

Over the following months, it seemed that all I encountered were Josh's excuses about schedule complications, but I have since come to realize that when a man truly cares for a woman, he will make the time to see her.

After months of vague quasi interest, I finally confronted Josh about his lack of communication with me, and that turned out to be the beginning of the end. Why, oh why, did I not just "click" away with my dignity intact? Did I really use guilt tactics? These pointless emails were like the last nails being pounded into the coffin of the relationship I was hoping would develop:

ME: ... As far as getting together, I am going to let you call me if you want to keep in contact. You have my number and know how to reach me - I leave a week from today.

Hope you have a good day...

Me **AGAIN:** Ok - I can see that you have decided not to write me back. It is odd to me that we go out once, you kiss me, then email me but never call me again, then tell me you want to be friends and then drop contact. Just for the record you could be honest with a girl and just say, "You know what? I just felt like kissing someone, not interested in being friends, take care." Just a thought.

Looking back at this last email I cringe. How could I have continued to pursue something with this dashing, dating deadbeat? It was like I was taking a gash and exposing it, and then every perceived rejection was Josh rubbing salt in the gaping wound. It is still embarrassing to me that I was so naïve, and foolishly hopeful, in light of his blatant disinterest. I chalk it up to the fact that almost any man, up to that point, who had kissed me, had wanted to start an exclusive relationship. That is what I knew, and I couldn't seem to reconcile that we shared such a powerful attraction (both physical and emotional), and that it was not headed anywhere. And so it continued:

JOSH: Yes, you are right Karen. I dropped the ball on writing and calling. I keep telling myself to get the number off the email and always forget to. As far as writing you back, I've been spending all my days in the lab and today and tomorrow we have presentations for the research. So, I spent the whole day listening to presentations in front of doctors.

The kissing part....well Karen you are absolutely right. I went out with you, had a great time, we kissed and the evening was great. Since then I left my job, started summer school and started research. Do I have time to call and write, absolutely. I stink at that and I dropped the ball. I've been a horrible, horrible friend, but I swear it was never a "needed someone to kiss-good bye" thing. I've just sucked at communicating.

You're a good person and don't deserve that. I apologize and sincerely hope that you find it in your heart to forgive me for being absent minded and inconsiderate. I will keep writing and gosh darnet, will find your number on the email to call you. Sorry about everything.

The fact that he couldn't seem to remember to "get my number off his email" should have been the writing on the wall for me. With his demanding schedule, Josh finally arranged our follow-up date, **which was almost a year to the day that we had first gone out.** Anyone with half a brain would have realized by now that if it takes a guy a year to go out on a second date with you, he is probably not interested. Nevertheless, I was already trapped in a place of delusional longing, and held onto the dream that we still had a chance.

I remember dining with him at a great steak house, as my crush on him resurfaced with a <u>vengeance</u>. Of course, when this date was over, it was the same old drill - barely communicating at all unless we happened to run into each other online. At least this time, he mercifully knew better than to kiss me. Disappointed with the blaring friend vibe present on the date, I hesitantly accepted the reality that I had been, up to that point, so expertly avoiding.

Finally, I got an inevitable email from Josh several months later letting me know that he must apparently have had enough spare time to date someone else, not casually, but seriously enough that his engagement was imminent:

JOSH: That's fantastic about the masters program. Yes, that's true about talking once a year. Much has happened since we've talked last. Last January '06, I recommitted my heart and life to Jesus, effectively ending my misery and loneliness. I went back to my old church where I had burned many bridges and it was a humbling experience. I've **grown so much since then. I am so happy and fulfilled.**

That's just the beginning...10 months after being back God placed a wonderful woman into my life. We are in a courting relationship right now, and have been for approximately 6 months. God really knew what he was doing in this match because we are so compatible! I can honestly say that I am so deeply in love with her, and soon I will be asking her to marry me. I'll be graduating from UTEP in May and I will start teaching (hopefully) for a while until she graduates, then I'll follow God's will and calling for my life. I hope to apply to the Texas Tech Physician Program, but it all depends on my calling.

Well you got paragraphs out of me, a great accomplishment! Take care Karen, Happy Easter and say hello to Ol' Canada for me!

Note how he softened the blow by casually giving me a general update on his life, and dropped the bomb near the end of the email? Tying his letter up with compliments and a polite though slightly patronizing wish that I would be well slammed yet another door with a finality of goodbye. If I had read the book by Greg Behrendt and Liz Tuccillo, He is Just Not That Into You, I would not have held on with even a sliver of hope for as long as I did.

Ladies, you might have felt that you've also had the best first date in your entire life, but the true chances of a possible romance depend on the timely follow-through of your new man. A tirade of excuses or just a general lack of pursuit is a very clear-cut answer to your query as to whether he is interested in you or not! At that time, I felt that I deserved some sort of answer for why we went from 60-0 in no time.

With no way of getting that closure, I finally had come to the conclusion that I was not going to get that concrete answer from Josh that I desired. Maybe he wouldn't have even been able to pinpoint the exact grounds for why we wouldn't have worked out long-term, and even if he would've been able to, would any explanation have been information that I'd really want to hear? Was there anything Josh could have expressed to me that would have satisfied my heart, which had been set on exploring a relationship with him? Ladies, it is like playing poker. You've got to know when to fold, and to recognize when the hand is dismal and unredeemable.

.... ;-)

All Talk, No Action Guys: You'll Never Actually Meet Them!

They're cute, they're employed, they know how to use the words "there", "their", and "they're" properly, so let's respond and see what happens.

This is a category of cyber men that needs to be addressed as a group, and from what I have heard from other online daters, (as well as experienced myself) these types of guys are a dime a dozen. You receive a wink or a message from someone who appears to be interested. "Hmmmmmm…" you think. They're cute, they're employed, they know how to use the words "there", "their", and "they're" properly, so let's respond and see what happens. It appears that there is a degree of fascination with you, as they are making the effort to chat, email, view your profile, send flirts, yet… they never actually suggest getting together for dinner, coffee, or any other type of meeting. This behavior is even more suspect if you both live in the same area, within driving distance of each other.

I am convinced that there are several reasons for this: One, they are married or taken, but just enjoy flirting with single girls. Two, that they have misrepresented themselves and know the illusion of who you think they are versus who they actually are will be shattered upon meeting, and they will end up being rejected. Three, they are shy and uncomfortable with the idea of a face-to-face encounter, so they put it off indefinitely.

Reasons that could be deemed acceptable would be those such as business trips or other out of town endeavors, as well as deadlines at work that end within a couple of weeks. Reasons that are not acceptable would be that they are just too busy, for the foreseeable future, with work, family, and hobbies. If they are so occupied, then why are they trying to cyber date?

True confessions here. I have used that generally busy excuse myself, but typically because I was still not sure that the guy was my type, or that I seriously wanted to meet him.

The bottom line is that if you are conversing with an online suitor and he is unnecessarily putting off a rendezvous, then you might want to move on to a real contender.

············ ;-)

Dan: International Man Of Mystery

> **Also he made a point of mentioning that no one would ever be able to track him down via the Internet; that he had "made sure of that". Hmmmmmm. Why would keeping his identity hidden be so important?**

Dan entered my life via the, supposedly very reliable, eHarmony venue. You have all seen the commercials on TV. The really good-looking couples and the ones that are at least at the same attractiveness level, gushing on how they are now complete since they met. Cheek kiss, arm caress, hug, and CUT! Pretty convincing ads though, as there are millions of singles grasping at this site like it is a life line being offered to escape their dreaded singleness. One of the catchy lines is "What if the person of your dreams is just a click away?" The seemingly snotty insinuation is that if one is solo; it is just because you are too lazy to look for that true love!

This is the site that does not allow you to search for matches, but based on an extensive personality/compatibility test, they decide that they know better than you do, what will work for you. Now, I can actually see the reasoning behind their argument, because if I was so great at picking my own prospects, I would probably be married by now! This site also keeps you from being able to view the profile photos until a certain point in the communication has been reached. I found this feature to be extremely frustrating. Do the eHarmony creators think that I have time to communicate with countless men, only to find that the majority of these men were not even remotely attractive to me? Chemistry is crucial, but even while believing this; I was willing to see if there was anything to being paired up solely based on personality traits and common beliefs, goals, and life visions.

With that being said however, I still do not quite see at the end of the day how a single woman with no children was paired up with an older, divorced man with four children. I have always been more comfortable in relatively large sized cities, while this guy was more comfortable in places where your nearest neighbors were twenty miles away.

Why did I even entertain this potential match once I had spoken to him on the phone a few times? I hesitate to give my true reason, as it sounds so incredibly feeble, but the urge to confess so that others learn from my mistake is overwhelming!

It was his southern Texas drawl. I wish I was kidding, but that deep, sexy voice made everyday words sound so masculine and sensual. Dan's accent had successfully distracted me from the fact that we probably had nothing in common. We have all made potential relationship justifications, haven't we?

In this case, mine was based on the successful marriage of one of my best friends. Jennifer and her husband don't really share many of the same interests, yet they are insanely happy. He hunts and fishes at every opportunity, and she is a hard-core vegetarian. This rationalization was just another way of excusing the already surfacing differences between Dan and me.

In the beginning, our conversations and dialogues were comfortable and entertaining. Then started the first hints of intrigue. There were the odd times I wondered aloud during our phone calls how I was going to be able to do something, whether at work or in my personal life, and this guy would matter-of-factly state things like, "All I have to do is tell them who I am, and it will be done immediately."

I kept asking him, "Who are you that you have that kind of power?" But he would never tell me.

With immigration issues it was the same thing - Dan would insist, "Forget all of the lawyer crap. I will just make one phone call and you will be a citizen, no questions asked." With all of these claims, I was unsure why he was not able to acquire custody of his 4 children, when he described his ex wife as a certifiable nut job!

Before Dan came out to El Paso for a visit, he said that he was going to fill me in on his spiritual side. He had to wait until then because the stories were ones that he would need to feel comfortable enough to tell me about in person. As you have probably surmised by now, spiritual beliefs are vital for me. In fact, I could never be serious with someone until I had made sure that this is set, and that we are compatible in this way. Walt had alluded to the fact that he "didn't just believe what he had been told", and had "done a lot of research" on the Bible and other things related to spirituality.

Please do not think that I have not had doubts and questions about my own faith. Everyone has. It is admirable to research the answers to the inquiries that one has. When I came out and specifically asked Dan if he thought the Bible was valid, his response was, "Which bible are you talking about?"

What kind of answer is that? All his responses seemed to take on a deflective question form, which had me wondering what he might have been trying to hide.

Looking back now, I wonder if Dan had a Superman complex. Everyone who really knows me is aware that my dream is to own a dog or two (I would today, but the owner of the property where I live does not allow pets under any circumstances). When I mentioned this, Dan brazenly informed me, "Just get this woman in the same place with me, and you will see that she will be convinced to let you have a dog." I chortled openly at him, explaining how he had no idea how much she opposed this, but he confidently retorted, "It is true - as soon as she finds out WHO I AM, it will no longer be a problem."

OK, was this guy a spy? A war hero? A high level CIA agent? What? I was so confused. He showed me his driver's license voluntarily, but still tried to imply that there was more than what he was showing me. Occasionally I would teasingly ask, with slight trepidation, "Who are you really, Dan?"

He refused to divulge, only mentioning, "Later on if you need to know, you'll know then." I would have been scared of him except that on his visit he was a truly nice person, who was a great guest, both agreeable and easy to please.

Another thing that seemed peculiar was that about a week before he came out to visit, he had "googled" me. Then he told me that he had found a lot of sites that I was on, that in fact I was "all over the Internet". Also, he made a point of mentioning that no one would ever be able to track him down via the Internet; that he had "made sure of that". Hmmmmmm. Why would keeping his identity hidden be so important?

The only reason I trusted him enough to hang out with him, was because we had spent hours and hours together every day on the phone. Despite this baffling behavior, he was as respectful and considerate as could be. There was a real dichotomy to Dan: On one hand he was the down home country boy, who liked to go huntin' and fishin'. He was the guy who had smeared deer blood on his kid's forehead after their first deer kill. On the other hand, he was the mysterious, intriguing, but vague man who apparently had powerful connections, and out rightly refused to tell me who he really was. So which was it? Who EXACTLY was he?

In the end, Dan came out to El Paso, and I got to sample the country boy with a dash of the fascinating, enigmatic man. Although we had fun together, I know he sensed that I likely would not be willing to give up my life to follow him to the ends of the earth, otherwise known as Small Town, Texas.

Although I have no problem with hunting or fishing, (my dad does both), I could not see myself conking a fish on the head, leading to its demise. I could barely watch Bambie, so I might faint at the sight of deer blood, moose blood, or any animal blood for that matter. In fact he even observantly told me that he was fairly sure that I did not like him as much as he liked me (which was true). Then Dan left, and I still don't know who he was, or where he had obtained all his "power". I will likely never find out the answers to my lingering questions about this one.

.... ;=)

Cesar: Alpha Male FBI Agent

> **I didn't grace his cruel observations with responses, thinking that this should be a forceful hint to stop. Instead this oaf found even more unkind comments to make. Though none of these comments were directed at me, it felt as though stinky trash was trickling out of his mouth.**

Cesar was one of those guys you meet online who seems like the macho player type, but one who could potentially have a big heart deep down. Being an FBI agent for a living, he kept weird hours and it was hard to set up our first date. Finally, we arranged to meet at Barnes and Noble for coffee. Sometimes I wondered if the baristas ever gossiped about how many different guys I had walked in with. With a hopeful mindset, I arrived early and took a seat.

While enthralled by my favorite magazines, I heard a deep voice address me, "Are you Karen?" This man was one of the tallest guys I had ever gone out with, and he was undeniably attractive. After shooting the breeze for a few minutes, I noticed that Cesar would make fun of people and how they looked. I didn't grace his cruel observations with responses, thinking that this should be a forceful hint to stop. Instead this oaf found even more unkind comments to make. Though none of these comments were directed at me, it felt as though stinky trash was trickling out of his mouth. (So far I was not seeing evidence of a potentially big heart deep down)

About fifteen minutes into this date, I arose and let Cesar know that I felt that we were not remotely compatible, and that I was going to leave. Now if you knew me and how much I loathe confrontation, you would have been truly impressed with my courage. After all, this confrontation could have ended up being a scene in my favorite coffee shop, where I was humiliated by a verbal bully.

Confused and surprised, he asked me why I wanted to cut the date short, so I told him that I do not find disparaging people to be a nice bonding experience, and that mocking individuals for not dressing well or other physical traits, made him very unattractive to me. Reaching for my purse, with every intention to split, Cesar pleaded with me to just wait for a minute and hear him out. Reluctantly, I sat down and he told me that he felt nervous, and admitted that he shouldn't have been putting people down. Meekly he asked if I could give him another chance to show that he was not that kind of man, and so we did actually end up dating for awhile.

When we stopped seeing each other, it was not because of a blow out or fight, but due to the recognition that we wanted different things in life. What I learned through my experience with this "alpha" male, is that sometimes guys will put up a bravado or tough front in the beginning, and it is ok to call them out on it, and give them a chance to show who they really are. Nerves and first date jitters can conceal the potential that a blind date may have, and underneath those anxious put downs, could be someone with a great heart.

.... ;-)

Military: Just Passing Through Guys

"One night or a wife," I was once told by a slightly inebriated young private at a local watering hole, "but not a lot in between."

El Paso is one of those cities that have a fairly large military population due to the location of Fort Bliss, where many young soldiers are stationed. Single girls out there may be assuming that this means a grand influx of eligible single men. Yes....and no. Let me start off by saying that I appreciate those who serve in the military. I feel these men and women are brave, and in many ways selfless for the sacrifices they are making to protect this country's freedom. Please do not send me letters telling me that I am stereotyping, because I know that I am. Any groupings of certain types of men are a type of generalization or stereotyping. Of course, there are also many men who will not fit the mold I am about to describe. In my experience, it seems that military men are looking for either something really casual or very serious when it comes to their search for women. "One night or a wife," I was once told by a slightly inebriated young private at a local watering hole, "but not a lot in between."

One interesting night out, my adopted little sister, Colleen, and I went out to shoot some pool at a billiards place that happened to be fairly close to Fort Bliss. Joking around that we might run into some cute soldiers, we headed in and secured a pool table. Suddenly, I realized that a man I had gone on a date with from Match.com was playing a game directly to the right of our table! One of the ways I recognized him was that he was wearing the exact outfit he had worn on our date: A red shirt and dark denim jeans. After our initial date, he had wanted to get together and I had blown him off, knowing there had been no romantic connection. That now put me in an awkward situation, which I probably deserved for not just coming clean and being honest with him. Trying to avoid eye contact of any kind was undeniably a challenge.

Within 20 minutes, we had two clean-cut army men approach us and slap a few dollar bills on the table. They were challenging us to a game, and offering us the "advantage" of splitting up and playing with each of them. Smooth. Did I mention that both of them were obviously hammered? The only reasons we entertained them was because they were attractive, we were bored, and I always feel this compassion for soldiers who are displaced and probably feel lonesome. What does it hurt to be friendly, right? Little did we know that serious drama was coming; it was like an older version of middle school antics!

The two men, one obviously in his early twenties, and the other a little older were making us laugh. The younger soldier almost blew it with me by asking if Colleen was my daughter! His companion, Julio, who ended up being glued to me most of the night, had commented that he was glad that there was someone closer to his age to hang out with. When I asked his age, it turned out he was only 27 years old. Realizing that he had not overhead his clueless pal's earlier insult, I felt legitimately flattered.

Once Julio felt comfortable around us, he started acting crudely and saying raunchy sexual things, so I promptly put him in his place.

"You better knock it off with the sex talk, or you can take your dollar and walk," I scolded.

After apologizing profusely, he asked me in all seriousness when I would allow him the privilege of taking me on a real date! Instead of answering, "How about a week from never?" I just avoided the question. Just around the time he started losing patience, and wanted to pin me down on a day and place, a fist fight erupted on the other side of the pool hall! Apparently one of their anti-social soldier friends had bought some guy's girlfriend a drink. The altercation started with a string of cuss words, and then they were at each other's throats. Then, to my amazement, as Colleen and I were heading to the door to leave, the bouncer asked us to wait on the patio until the "other party" had left the vicinity. When my mild protest was ignored, and we were all led out the back door, I realized that I was in the equivalent of an adult "time out". This was unbelievable! We hadn't even come in with these guys, and were sent outside with them like badly behaved children for 10 minutes.

Thank goodness they hadn't calculated our "time out" using the typical equation of age= minutes in confinement. That in and of itself would've been more than a good reason to lie about my age!

After we were released, we headed outside, only to be confronted by one of the small punks (from the "other party") who had returned in his truck. Tired of listening to him spout off idle threats to three much bigger guys, I excused myself to go and have a heart-to-heart with my new friend, the bouncer.

"Look, one of the guys who was causing trouble is back and about to have the snot beat out of him," I patiently explained. Now this really was just like middle school, because students never fail to throw each other under the bus. "You may want to call the police if this kid doesn't depart the premises," I tattled.

"Thanks for not taking matters into your own hands," was his reply. As I walked away, shaking my head in disbelief, I realized that a lot of girls probably would have been entertained by these kind of bar fights. How sad. Colleen had thought the younger soldier was cute, but he was to be shipped out in less than two weeks, so it was an infatuation that was never meant to be. I, by this point, was even less interested in letting Julio take me out on a "real date".

You need to keep in mind when considering dating or marrying someone who has answered Uncle Sam's call, that you will probably be moving fairly often, and some sort of deployment is inevitable at any time. Are you someone who deals with radical, unexpected change well? Personally, I am adventurous, but I am someone who wholeheartedly steers clear of drastic change. When it comes down to my everyday life, I am all about consistency and familiarity. I also don't like the feeling that the military completely dictates many of the decisions of their soldiers. That lack of control makes me feel dizzy. Some people thrive on not knowing what lies ahead. Therefore, if you find true love with a soldier, (and there are a multitude of these men online) make sure that he is one of the spouse seekers, not a just a thrill seeker, and then weigh the pros and cons of entering into a relationship where the US government calls the shots.

.... ;-)

The Scammer: He's Not Who He Appears to Be

There are men who are preying on lonely women, knowing that they may be able to exploit them for their own gain.

From what I hear, this is surprisingly more common for men to encounter than women. The reason is likely because many men want to save the damsel in distress by being her hero. While we women have to endure the jerks who send one line emails asking if we would mind entertaining their odd fetishes, men have the issue of women who are trying to charm, and then scam them (usually going after their finances).

An underhanded scammer can try to pull the wool over women's eyes as well. I have received some very strange and elaborate emails from international men online. Typically, my radar goes off that something is amiss when they come on too strong, so I delete these notes and move on. My warning to you is that if someone is telling you something that sounds too unbelievable, than it probably is.

In recent years I have come across identical and lengthy emails sent to me by exceptionally handsome guys (usually including only one photo, which could have been retrieved anywhere off the internet). These messages usually begin with a lot of flowery sentiments about how I am one of the most beautiful ladies in the world. Really? Simply based on what photos I have posted on my profile? As healthy as I would like to think my self-esteem is, I am not delusional!

Then, the wordy notes continue with almost the exact same "sob story", where these men are widowed, and are just looking for that one fantastic woman who can complete their lives and help raise their children. If I had to guess how many of these almost identical types of emails I have received over the last few years, I would say there were at least 30 of them.

A part of me wants to respond and see how they would try to draw me in, so I would be familiar with what their game is. The reason I don't is because it would obviously be a waste of time and energy, both of which I need to conserve for my everyday life! There are men who are preying on lonely women, knowing that they may be able to exploit them for their own gain. Maybe they want a green card. Maybe they have a personality disorder, and just like to play with a woman's emotions. Maybe they want a sugar mama. If someone ever asks you to wire money or anything else similarly scandalous, report him or her immediately to the site on which you met. Then make sure to block these people from being able to contact you in the future.

.... ;-)

Ricardo: Proposed to Me Within 24 Hours

At this point we had known each other for well under 24 hours. As the words inexplicably started to tumble out, I believe I whispered something like, "Don't you think we would need to know each other a lot better before we tackle a question like that one?"

Ricardo Moreno. I met him on a Christian matchmaking website, and we chatted on the site a few times. We became Facebook friends and kept things casual. After an appropriate amount of time, he asked if he could come out and visit me in El Paso, and I told him that was a great idea. He was living in a small city in the Texas panhandle, making El Paso look like a raging metropolis. What I especially appreciated about this visit was that it started on a Saturday, and it was the day after school was officially over for the year! Already, I was feeling an incredible air of freedom and knew that when he went home, I didn't have to frantically get lessons planned for Monday.

As a rule when picking up someone at the airport who I have talked to online, I feel extremely nervous. With Ricardo though, we had more spoken like we were friends who could be interested in each other, rather than participating in the usual open flirting that commonly takes place on the phone. I didn't feel the kind of pressure that would have normally accompanied this situation.

I waited for him to appear at the bottom of the escalator in the airport, and kept wondering things like, "Does he look like his picture?" "Will we get along for an entire weekend?" and, "Will he think I am attractive?" I immediately recognized him (This was a positive, because this meant he had not tried to misrepresent himself). In fact, Ricardo looked better in person than he did in his pictures.

Whenever I have been in this "internet suitor coming to visit me" situation, it has always been the same. There are the first critical few minutes where both parties are trying to see if there is any physical chemistry. If you feel it, then right away you wonder if they feel the same. If you don't, you wonder if, and kind of hope, they don't as well. With Ricardo, I just relaxed and treated him like he was an old guy friend visiting me from out of town. Although there was an attraction between us, I was not sure that we had the same ideas about faith in God, which is a deal breaker for me. After checking in, and dropping off his things at the hotel, we went out for lunch and had a great talk. Ricardo was comical without trying too hard, could keep up his end of the conversation, and seemed genuinely respectable.

Next on our agenda, was a walk with the dogs belonging to my personal trainer, Sally. This killed two birds with one stone - first he would get to meet some people I knew, and I could see if the "girls" approved (dogs are great judges of character). Secondly, I have always enjoyed being active in an outdoor setting, and I wanted to see if Ricardo would also enjoy this kind of leisure.

Everything was going according to plan, when I suddenly got a flat tire! Luckily, I pulled over right in front of a car dealership, and after sweet-talking the guy in charge; we managed to get a jack, and were able to attach the spare. Again Ricardo earned some "points" for being patient and easygoing. We proceeded to a tire shop, and while they were putting on new tires, we had a drink in a little café nearby. At this point, I was unsure of whether there would be a romantic connection or not, but at least this was turning out to be a fun-filled weekend!

One hundred and fifty dollars and two new tires later, we made our way over to pick up the pooches. About midway through our walk, Ricardo pulled me close to him with his hand around my waist. Then right there on the jogging trail, he planted a kiss on me. I would like to say this was like a scene from a romantic movie, but that kiss was SLOBBERY. My heart dropped, but I was not ready to give up without a fight. Later, I can honestly say I attribute that one instance of bad kissing to him being overeager and nervous, because he greatly improved as the weekend continued.

That night, Ricardo and I went to one of my favorite dive bars where they have karaoke every Saturday. There were a lot of wanna be rock stars there, and it was fun to watch and listen to all the confident, tone-deaf singers who had just utilized their liquid courage. We were very cozy and obviously together, and it was like Ricardo couldn't take his eyes off of me the entire evening. When we had listened to enough of the off-key singing, I was going to drop him off, but decided to join him for awhile to talk. Of course, he wanted things to become more romantic, which was fine with me since I had already made it crystal clear that I was not going to sleep with him.

When it was about time for me to go home, he suddenly grabbed me and declared, "I think we should get married. Let's just do it! What do you think?" Alarmingly, he mistook my speechlessness as a possible sign of agreement. I shook my head, wondering if I had heard him correctly. At this point we had known each other for well under 24 hours. As the words inexplicably started to tumble out, I believe I whispered something like, "Don't you think we would need to know each other a lot better before we tackle a question like that one?"

His answers are a blur to me now, but I believe phrases like, "Sometimes you just know when something feels right!", "I think we would be so great together!", and "Let's just go for it!" were exclaimed. My carefully crafted response was that we had enjoyed a great FIRST day together, and that we would talk more about this when he was sober. He adamantly insisted that this was how he felt, and that this feeling would not change the next day. Not wanting to further hurt Ricardo's feelings, and thinking that maybe it was the Jack Daniels talking, I just kissed him goodnight and left.

The next morning I was to give him a ride to the airport, and figured that when we met up, and he was no longer under the influence, things would be back to normal. Still not sure whether this was destined to be a lasting romantic relationship or not, I figured that this issue would work itself out, and decided not to worry about it.

Usually I am on time, especially when my task is to get someone to their expensive, non-refundable flight. For some reason on this particular morning, I was confused about the time I needed to be at the hotel to pick up Ricardo.

When I suddenly received a hysterical phone call from him, demanding to know why I had not shown up at his door, I knew I'd messed up. Apparently, the time I had thought I would need to pick him up, was the time he was supposed to BE at the airport. At the risk of receiving an expensive speeding ticket, I arrived at his hotel, whisked him to the airport, and he made it to his flight. However, some major toddler-like pouting took place on the way there.

If truth be told, I was glad to see this part of Ricardo's character revealed, because it just confirmed to me the immaturity I had suspected when he had declared his undying love for me the night before. Proposing on the first date is not romantic, my friends. Beware of that kind of unwarranted, and more than slightly inappropriate, gesture. As it turned out, Ricardo and I stayed friends for awhile, but when I did not eagerly return his sentiments, eventually he defriended me on Facebook, probably at the request of the next girl to whom he proposed.

Unexpected Update: Almost a year and half after this event occurred, I ran into Ricardo on the same site where we'd met while taking advantage of one of their 3 day free trials. (See Online Tips Section for more about free trials).

Ricardo immediately started to instant message me, and proceeded to inform me that I had broken his heart. According to him, I had been his girlfriend and had dumped him. When I debated this fact, he seemed a tad perplexed. He then proceeded to tell me that he had thought my boyfriend at the time, whom he had seen on Facebook, was ugly and not nearly as good looking as him. Not sure how to react to that revelation, I steered the conversation to safer waters such as work and school. Because I had not chosen my wedding dress, created a reception guest list, or hired a wedding planner, I finished the conversation with him, and moved on to communicating with other men who could suitably pace themselves when embarking on a relationship.

.... ;-)

Tim: Enough of the Bachelor Life, I Want Babies!

> I could almost see him doing the mental calculations (he was a number cruncher) of how long we would have to date before getting married, and then how long before we would start trying to have kids. Wasn't it usually the woman who thought about this stuff? This is what all those romantic comedies would lead us to believe, but I have come to the conclusion that many men have their own "kiddie clocks" ticking away; some to the point that the hands are almost spinning out of control.

I am positive that if you are a woman in your thirties or forties, you are going to encounter this particular specimen in the online dating arena. After running into Tim on Match.com, it did not take him long to get down to business and ask me to meet up with him for coffee. As the school year was coming to a close, I decided to give it a go before heading back up to Canada. Worst case scenario was that if the date didn't turn out well, being out of the country for a few months would be a successful way to "fade away" slowly without hurting his feelings. Best case scenario was that if we hit it off, when I got back (if we were both still on the market) we could actually start seeing each other.

We met up at my second favorite Starbucks, and this time, I arrived before he did. This was to be a monumental date for me, since I never go out with blonde men. When asked why this is, it is hard to formulate a credible, sane reason, except that I am normally not attracted to them in the slightest. This preference has been ingrained since I was young. Maybe that little heartbreaker blonde boy, Mark Mason, who I had a crush on in 3rd grade was the cause for this aversion. I'd loved him so much, but alas, he'd been enamored with the prettiest and most popular girl in our class! At least he'd seemed head over heels for her in my imagination. Likely, he'd been spending most of his time making "zoom zoom" noises with his Hot Wheels, and creating galactic battleships with his Legos, rather than daydreaming about girls.

Regardless of this past trauma, I trudged on to make the attempt to get to know Tim. As I opened the door and did a quick scan of the room, I noticed that he was not yet there. Just as I was about to scope out a seat, across from a gentleman with an atrocious toupee, I heard my name being called in a cheerful, excited tone.

When going out on a blind date, the dream is that you will NOT run into anyone who knows you. Even though it shouldn't be embarrassing that you are sacrificing your time to meet someone you do not know, let's face it, it is. The last situation you want to find yourself in is that a friend or acquaintance bumps into you, just as you are meeting up with Mr. Possibly. Even though I logically know that I shouldn't be ashamed of dating Internet guys, it is still hard to shake the stigma attached to this situation.

Looking toward the direction of the voice calling out my name, I suddenly realized that it was my friend Lori. If I was destined to endure any familiar encounter at this uncomfortable moment, I was elated that it was with her. Lori is as sweet, caring, and genuine as they come. She'd been having coffee with a mutual friend, and so I quickly walked over to speak to them both. I was hoping to have completed a short catch up conversation with Lori, and then ease my way, incognito, into meeting Tim. Not meant to be. Before I could detangle myself from the short dialogue with Lori, he'd arrived and immediately recognized me. I had to excuse myself, and I admit that I made it appear as if Tim was a legitimate friend of mine. Later I came clean with Lori, but at that moment, I didn't want to feel like I was being watched with the speculation of, "How are they getting along?" That would have simply been too much pressure!

I carried this off well, and when Lori started to leave Starbucks, she came up to say goodbye. I calmly executed what I deem the "vague introduction" technique. This is where I do not reveal how I know someone, but do my duty in providing his or her name. After Lori's stage left exit, we'd carried on with our nonstop banter. While some men are hard to engage in an enjoyable tête-à-tête, Tim was more than able to hold his own.

Before I knew it, the coffee cups were empty, and a few hours had painlessly passed. We had tackled most of the first date topics, and the only oddity I had discovered was the way he'd talked about his niece and nephew. In my mind, there are no children cuter than my own niece and nephew, who I have affectionately nicknamed Jefe and Mamacita. (English translation: Boss and Little Mama) So, obviously, if anyone can relate to someone who adores the little tykes in the family, it would be me. However, something different was going on. The tone of his voice presented such an intense yearning, that I immediately sensed that this man desperately wanted, no NEEDED, to have his own babies as soon as possible. Being older than 35 at the time of this date, I was not entirely confident that I was meant to have children of my own. Without a doubt, I would've considered adoption under the right circumstances, but at this point in my life, the idea of popping out a gaggle of children was not something that was even a desire of mine. Blonde and baby crazy. Two strikes.

After a few hours of being together, we tentatively planned a future date. We considered possibly hitting a museum or art show if it would work out before I was scheduled to leave for the summer. I knew that I was not being presumptuous in assuming that Tim had enjoyed my company. He'd even made the comment as he was leaving that he could have stayed and talked with me all day! It was whether he would follow through with further contact that was up in the air. As for whether I was interested or not, that was still up for consideration, as well. Broadening my horizons was a goal for dating that I had made, so I had decided to just wait and see what the future would bring.

We had a few more phone conversations, and shared some texts before I left. One of my biggest pet peeves is when a man texts me in the late morning to see if I can hang out that same afternoon. Unless he is a platonic friend or a long term boyfriend, it reeks of him assuming that I have nothing else going on. Tim tried this maneuver when attempting to set up our second date. Sure Tim, I wanted to drop everything I had planned for my day and disappoint any friends with whom I was scheduled to hang out, for a chance to grab a morsel of your time. How did you know? This date obviously wasn't happening. I refused to be one of those girls who continually put her friends on the backburner whenever she has something cooking with a new guy. Declining his offer, I suppose Tim felt insecure or slighted, because he did not try to ask me out again before I left.

Later that summer, when I was disembarking from my plane after a trip to the Dominican Republic, I did receive a text from Tim, just checking in to see how I was. An inquiry was also made as to when I would be returning to El Paso. Somehow, once I had returned to the hustle and bustle of life and work again, I'd completely forgotten about Tim. That is, until I'd received the following email:

TIM: Glad to hear your residency has been approved. So what options are you exploring? How was your summer? We should grab a drink sometime and you can tell me all about your summer. I remember you being easy to talk to and time seemed to fly. Hope all is well.

The texts commenced all over again, and finally I agreed to meet him on a chilly Friday night in the beginning of December. We met at an elegant place that still managed to feel comfortable and inviting. This get together had a completely different feel than so many of my other online connections, since

Tim and I had already met in person. A second date can be rare with cyber suitors.

Tim already knew what I looked like, knew my personality, knew about my morals and beliefs, and still wanted to hang out. This felt more like a true date than just another internet date, and I wasn't sure how I felt about that. He was a nice guy, but I wasn't sure there was enough personality connection to cement a passionate, exciting relationship. Clearly, I was still willing to give it a try, though. Otherwise, I would have been at home with some take-out, curled up on the couch with a blanket, watching something from Netflix.

I remember feeling some butterflies as I entered the restaurant, spotting Tim immediately. Winter fashion worked for him. He was wearing a sharp blazer, a stylish button down shirt that accentuated his blue eyes, and an exquisite pair of dark denim jeans. Don't even get me started on his shoes! Actually, that is the one part of the ensemble I don't recall, but I can safely remark that they matched the rest of this chic outfit.

The hug we shared felt natural. Tim's eyes were warm and welcoming, and I felt both attractive and special right from the beginning! A good start to a date. The next hour sped by as we caught up on what had been happening since our last meeting.

Tim had started dating someone he had met online 3 months earlier, and that is why he had been missing in action. They had broken up a few weeks before he'd called me. He sure hadn't taken a lot of time to lick his wounds before he'd gotten back up on the horse again, but he was obviously eager to saddle up with me. Gazing at me, Tim told me how great I looked for my age. I thanked him for the compliment and assured him that I'd always tried to take care of myself. Then he mentioned something, and although I do not remember his remark, it had something to do with me being 29 years old. Chuckling openly about that, my response was, "I think I remember being 29, but that was awhile ago!"

Tim looked confused. "What do mean?"

I laughed again, but could see he was serious, "Tim, I am 39 years old."

"I could have sworn you were 29," he sputtered, looking like he had just been sucker punched in the gut. I guess he had forgotten to look at that part of the profile. Even though it was a couple of years off, my age was not stated as being 29 years old! It is necessary to interject here that I had originally put the wrong birth date in the Match database when I'd first signed up, under the strong advisement of a friend. Her experience was that she had been hit on exclusively by men over fifty when she had posted 35 as her age. She'd said that it was ok to fudge a few years, as long as you explained your reasoning to the men right away, and revealed how old you really were. This was my policy, and I was sure I had let Tim know how old I was, but in my defense, even if I hadn't, it still said 34 years old on my profile.

To his credit, Tim made a deceptively quick recovery. However, the foreshadowing of our first coffee conversation, and how he'd gushed about his love for kids, returned to the forefront of my mind. I could almost see him doing the mental calculations (he was a number cruncher) of how long we would have to date before getting married, and then how long before we would start trying to have kids. Wasn't it usually the woman who thought about this stuff? This is what all those romantic comedies would lead us to believe, but I have come to the conclusion that many men have their own "kiddy clocks" ticking away; some to the point that the hands are almost spinning out of control.

The date continued, and we parted with a long hug and a kiss on the cheek. It had been a great time, but I was not betting the farm that we would ever go out again. So you can imagine my surprise the next day when I received a text asking if I would be free to go see a movie with him that very night. I confidently concluded that he was interested in me. Things were moving along. Little did I know how quickly they would take a turn for the worse.

Tim had mentioned, in passing, that he had let his Match.com account expire, and hadn't been on it for a few months. In the short time that we had been hanging out, I hadn't been visiting the site either. One night, I received a biweekly email at my hotmail address that included the profiles of possible men who might be matches for me. To my surprise, Tim's photo was staring at me. He had purposefully subscribed to Match.com once again?! Dating me had sent him sprinting back to seek love in cyberspace? I am not going to lie - it was a forceful blow to my ego.

When he sent me a flirty text a few hours later, I was torn as to whether I should mention that I knew he had joined Match again, or not. Maybe it came back to the fact that I was not very attracted to blondes. Or maybe I was tired of game play. Within a few minutes, I dropped the bomb. He freaked out (even obvious via text messages), and tried to back pedal, commenting on how he wished I was there to cuddle with him.

Then he informed me that he knew I was the type of girl that needed a serious relationship, and he wasn't sure if he could offer that to me. I replied by letting him know that I didn't know if I would even be interested in a romance with him, as we had only been out on two dates. At the end of the texting marathon, I told him I didn't think we would work out. When a guy starts dating me, and AFTER that joins a dating website, it is time to bail!

I hope he finds a sweet 20-something year old with great childbearing hips who is looking for a baby daddy. Then he can get some use out of the Babies "R" Us sales fliers that I know are lying around in his car!

.... ;-)

ADHD Guy: Way Over the Top

> Avoiding IMs, avoiding texts, avoiding emails. I was starting to wonder if I was going to need to grow accustomed to a life on the run. Should I dye my hair? Get a big dog? Purchase colored contacts maybe?

Craig initially contacted me on Match.com with an email that smacked me like a gigantic runaway snowball gathering more momentum as it sped along its path. His thoughts were all over the place, and it was hard to follow what he was trying to say. Maybe he was just in a hurry, I'd thought. He was fairly attractive, and his profile said he was Christian/Other, so I figured it would be worthwhile to communicate with him and see if the situation would improve.

In follow up emails, he would throw in some really odd comments, which were truly inappropriate. For example, he spoke about one online date on which he had been, where he took a friend along. That way, if the woman would not have been pretty enough for him, he could have dumped her off on his less picky friend, who could play on her feelings of rejection to try to score. That poor girl! I never did find out if she made the cut or not, because by then, this erratic behavior had overwhelmed me, and I was retreating. How dense was this guy that he was confessing his dating sins to someone he was hoping to take out?

Avoiding IMs, avoiding texts, avoiding emails. I was starting to wonder if I was going to need to grow accustomed to a life on the run. Should I dye my hair? Get a big dog? Purchase colored contacts maybe? After a few days of not responding to any of Craig's attempts at contact, he sent a bizarre video directly to my phone, where he pleaded with me to reach out to him. Then, he proceeded to ask via this mini-media production, what he had done to be on my "sh*@ list?" I hadn't known this man well enough for him to have made any kind of list!

Ladies, when a man contacts you, acts inappropriately right away, and doesn't seem to be able to pull it together, it is better to walk away, just in case whatever crazy bug he has is contagious!

.... ;-)

Jared: Just Give Me a Side Order Of Crazy Ex Girlfriend

It is only a matter of time before she finds me, I thought. Memories of those really creepy Lifetime movies started to flicker in my mind, and that was when I knew that no matter what happened I needed to flee from this situation. I could almost imagine the sinister score of music playing in the background. At this point in the movie you would tell the seemingly clueless protagonist to get out and run for her life.

Ok young single women everywhere… Let the following account be a warning to you. Every once and awhile you are going to be put in a position where you will encounter that guy who almost seems too good to be true. Before jumping into anything, there is a question that you need to ask, and that question would be, "Is he connected to a crazy b%@**h who is going to harass me with constant emails and incessant phone calls?"

Now, the tricky part to this scenario is that the guy is likely NOT going to be upfront and volunteer this information. He knows that it is a turnoff and is trying to impress you. Instead of coming clean, he will reel you in with discussing how family oriented he is, how he has a great job that he loves, how he helps little old ladies cross the street, and enjoys rescuing lab puppies from the pound. My daddy told me that if something appears too good to be true, it usually is.

Here is an example of a typical, breezy email that too-good-to-be-true Jared sent before the tornado of a fanatical ex girlfriend hit the scene. Note the references to family closeness and general well-roundedness to lure me in:

```
JARED:    Hey Chica!
          Yesterday was my first day back to work. I was totally
          hurting by noon after my weight lifting session...lol!
          Anyways....no I have never been to Canada, but I would love
          to go if I was invited. (hint hint)

          Some good friends of mine drove into ABQ to visit me for a
          few days. We had tons of fun!

          For the 4th, my family and I went camping for a few days,
          watched the fireworks on the lake, then we went to a Dude
          Ranch on our last day. We were all a little hesitant about it
          at first, since it was a spare of the moment type thing, but
          we all ended up having a blast. We "pigged-out" and
          karaoked....LOL! Other than that, I have been a good boy.....
```

Before I returned to Canada for the summer, I was tossing around the idea of going to visit Jared in Albuquerque. It is a quick and easy drive - only four hours, and part of me did not want to keep this "online flirtation" fueled over a whole summer, only to discover that we were not right for each other. I was bored since school was out, just waiting for my flight the following week, and there I was, ready to just get in the car and drive. I had thought about even calling my friend Jessica who lives in Albuquerque to let her know I would be arriving late that night.

Being spontaneous can be a positive thing, but sometimes I can take it too far, and not think through a situation logically.

Suddenly, I was online booking a hotel. My suitcase was out and I was throwing clothes and toiletries in while trying to remember if there was gas in the car. "When was the last time I checked my oil?" I wondered. I could clearly hear my mother's disapproving commentary running through my head, as I threw my bag into the trunk of my 1996 Honda Civic. "Karen Rissling, why in the world are you willing to chase down a man who lives four hours away? Don't you think he should be the one making the trip, instead of you? Do you want to look desperate?" Ignoring her imaginary advice, I justified the trip to myself by saying that I would also be visiting with my close friend Jessica, who I rarely get to see, and who had been the one to make the last few trips down to El Paso.

Just when I was about to depart, it started to rain. Not a big deal right? If you lived in El Paso, you would understand that it is a rare occurrence for it to even drizzle, so this downpour was completely unexpected. The rain was coming down so hard that I could barely make out the road right in front of me. Convinced it would stop in five or ten minutes like it usually does, and ignoring this obvious omen, I continued on my trek.

This road trip from hell was dicey right from the beginning. Between the lack of visibility and the obvious hydroplaning, I should have turned around in the first twenty minutes. Friends will vouch for the fact that I am determined and stubborn. I had booked a room! I had made my sloppy arrangements, and needed to plod ahead. I had no intention of letting this relationship continue over the course of the summer to discover finally that it was another dead end. As they say, curiosity can kill the cat, or at the very least, get the cat into a serious wreck. Did I mention that in my rush to leave, I had written down the directions to Albuquerque, but that I had not looked at them carefully?

Singing along to my MP3, at last, the rain lightened up to a mere sprinkle, and the tension in my shoulders and body started to loosen up. After I had been driving for well over two hours, I called Jessica to say hi before it got too late. When she asked me where I was, I cheerfully read her the name of the town I had just passed. "Karen, you're joking right?" she anxiously inquired.

"No Jess, why?"

"Karen, didn't you take the exit on the outskirts of Las Cruces?"

"I was supposed to go that way?"

"Hold on Karen, let me get online." A minute or so went by. At this point, my cell phone battery was dying because I had not charged it, due to the fact that I had not been planning to make this trip. Thanks a lot impulsivity! My phone was down to just one bar of power. Finally, Jessica was back to break the bad news.

"I don't know how to tell you this Karen, but you are really close....to Tucson, Arizona."

"Noooooooooo!" I howled, "Are you kidding? Please say you are kidding!"

"You would need to turn around now, and head all the way back to Las Cruces. Then it will be over 3 more hours from there."

At this point, I might have persevered, except that A) I was exhausted. B) I knew that it was foolish for a woman to be attempting a trip this far in a vehicle as old as mine, without a working cell phone, and C) Part of me was beginning to wonder if God was trying to save me from myself and keep me from meeting this gentleman.

Needless to say, I went home to Canada for the summer, without meeting fun-loving Jared from Albuquerque. What started as an innocent flirtation quickly became a messy situation from which I spent most of my vacation attempting to untangle myself.

The first sign that something was strange happened on a normal evening. While visiting my brother's family, I had left my cell phone in the room where my dad and brother were playing online poker. When they came in to watch TV, my brother happened to mention how my phone had been ringing constantly. In fact, because of my ringtone, he had been able to memorize the lyrics to "Halo" by Beyonce, even though he is more of a classic rock connoisseur. Out of curiosity, I checked my phone, and noticed that I had 12 missed messages from a PRIVATE number. That's weird, I thought. Who would be trying to contact me and block the number? Trust me when I say that none of the people with whom I choose to associate would call me repeatedly without leaving messages.

Warning bells started going off in my head. A few days later a phone call from Jared solidified what I thought was happening. Finally, after a lifetime of avoiding this time of entanglement, I had walked into the situation of being interested in a guy with a side order of lunatic. According to him, his 12 year old son noticed that he had been talking to a woman fairly often, and went snooping through his phone with the mission of getting my name and number to pass on to his deranged and unbalanced mother.

Enter the mother, who will be referred to in this ditty as "Psycho". Not wanting to deal with this woman head on, I ignored the calls. At this point, Jared "fessed up" that she had chased off several girls, and that he was going to have to do something about it. He then reassured me that this behavior would stop, but that he would understand if I wanted to drop off of the scene. I had not even met Jared yet, and probably should have just gone ahead and brought the hatchet down severing all ties, but I didn't have the heart. Also, I just wanted to enjoy my vacation and not be drawn into some big soap opera drama.

Less than a week later, while in the Dominican Republic enjoying paradise, I checked my email and discovered that some stranger claiming to be a friend of Jared's ex had written me messages on both Facebook and Myspace. Under closer inspection, I realized that this mystery girl had joined these venues for the pure intent of reaching me, unless she really only had one friend, no personal info, or pictures. This "Melissa", who Jared still claims he does not know, blasted his character on every level. From stories of how he made his ex get abortions since he was not ready to become a dad, to how he had been charged with cases of domestic violence, these accusations were both shocking and confusing. Here are some of the disturbing emails that I received from Jared's ex girlfriend, who I am sure was masquerading as "Melissa" in order to communicate with me. Keep in mind that I have not included SEVERAL of the emails:

PSYCHO EX: Hi Karen,

>My name is Melissa. I've known Cecelia and Jared a long time. I sent you a message on your Facebook account, however, I'm not sure which account you check more frequently - so I thought I'd send the same message here. I just wanted to send you a warning about Jared. I typically don't do this sort of thing, but.... I really think someone should be truthful to you about him. I have seen Cecelia struggle recently about Jared's involvement with you. I know Jared was sleeping with Cecelia......don't know when they stopped, or if they have - but I know she's really upset. They have two kids together and I know she has had great hopes that they work out their problems (I have my doubts). I do know that Jared has been very abusive with Cecelia throughout their relationship and still continues to try and control her every move. He has always made comments about knowing where her where abouts and how she is dressed.
>
>Jared is VERY CONTROLLING. I know Jared was arrested on two occasions for domestic violence on Cecelia. Believe me, Jared will deny it. **(Here there were paragraphs of legal terms and charges that were described at length, which I cannot include in this book).** This is REAL, please investigate it for yourself for your own safety with this individual. Jared has a way with words and his actions.....but he is NOT at all "great" person he portrays himself to be. Don't believe his lies, I'm sure he has already painted a pretty poor picture of Cecelia. I know Cecelia is struggling with him......but

it's real, and she has issues because of his continued abuse. Jared preys on honest, nice, and successful women and you appear to be just that. Good luck!!! E-mail me if you want any more info, I'm sure I can provide you with it.

ME: Hi Melissa,
It is strange to write someone that I do not know - but felt that I should try to. Right now I am on vacation overseas and so I only check my email sporadically.

First of all, I want you to know that I am not romantically involved with Jared - at this point we are only friends. I don't actually even know him that well. I am going to check out the information that you gave me when I get back - I appreciate that - if Jared is indeed who you are telling me he is, then I definitely will not continue the friendship. How do you know both Jared and Cecelia (I am assuming she is his ex - the mom of his two kids)?

If you have any more info that I can look up online about Jared, let me know - all that I have seen is that he seems educated, friendly, and nice - but I do not know him well.
Thanks,
Karen

P.S. I did get a bunch of missed calls on my cell phone from a private number - it was really unusual - do you know anything about that? I didn't receive a message.

PSYCHO EX: Hi Karen,

I'm really glad you took the time to reply to my e-mail. I typically don't get involved in someone else's relationship; however, I know what went on between the two of them. Jared has been telling Cecelia you are his girlfriend, and she has been so upset. Cecelia herself has really struggled getting over this guy. He tries to control her every move, he tries isolating her from her family and friends. I know Cecelia has recently started some therapy with a counselor, because she knows she has to get away from his abuse. I know I can get

copies of those police reports from Cecelia, and I will mail
them to you. I really think you should be EXTRA careful with
him.

I'm sure he told you he was an engineer, right? I found out
he has a degree in business administration. He also told
Cecelia many lies while he was with her. He told her he
played baseball for NMSU.......completely a lie again. I
think Cecelia has really been trying to make it work for
their kids. How did you meet Jared? Well, I know you probably
have things to do, just be cautious and if you want a copy of
those reports I'll mail them to you (only if you'd like). I
also know Cecelia would be more than happy to tell you what
kind of guy Jared is. I'll give her number if you want to
talk to her, I know she wouldn't mind. Have fun overseas and
be safe.

Cecelia's number is the following if you want to talk to her
505-***-**** (h) 505-***-**** (c)

PSYCHO EX AGAIN: Hi Karen,

So I asked Cecelia if she may have called you since you had
restricted calls. She told me she had and blocked the calls
because she is afraid you'll tell Jared she called you. Jared
has been threatening to take her to court constantly and she
just doesn't want him to have another thing to tell the
lawyers about. He has been taking Cecelia to court
constantly......I know she's really worried about finances
because of the fighting. I think that's why she tries so hard
to work it out with Jared. Jared has the attitude (if he
can't have her - no one can)- so he makes her life as
miserable as he can. Sorry, don't mean to go on and on about
Jared - but hope that answers your questions about the calls.
Please don't tell Jared about Cecelia calling you........it
will cause more problems than you know. I know Cecelia means
well by calling you.

ME: Hi Melissa,

I just got back from my trip - trying to see friends and family while I still can. I have been trying to look up the case numbers online and have not been able to find them. Is there a way that you could send me the link? I got quite a few messages from Cecelia, I believe, when I arrived back into Canada - at this time I do not feel comfortable talking to her...I am sure she is nice, but this whole situation over a developing FRIENDSHIP is a bit overwhelming to me.
She had mentioned in her message not to tell Jared she had called, and the only thing he knew was that his son had gotten my name off his phone and that must have been how she got my phone number. Before I got your first messages, I told him that I had received a bunch of calls from a private number but had not been there to pick up - also it costs me A LOT of money to use my phone here in Canada to the United States, so I don't carry it around like I would in the US. If you could send those specific links, that would help me out. Thanks

PSYCHO EX: Hi Karen,

I don't think Jared has been real honest about his relationship with Cecelia either. I think she's really upset about him even talking with you. I know she not upset with you..just with Jared -because he's playing games with her and trying to make her jealous with you. I know she still loves him. I don't think either of them are completely over each other. I just went with Cecelia on my lunch break to Planned Parenthood for the Plan B (emergency contraceptive pill) because she was with Jared last night. I think that's why she is so upset with your involvement with him, even if it is friendship (it's causing lots of problems between them).

They have a family together, and I know Cecelia wants them to re-build their relationship. I just want to let you know what's going on, don't believe everything Jared tells you. I KNOW he's not over Cecelia and vice versa. It is your choice, but if it was you in Cecelia's shoes trying to fight for her family wouldn't you understand her feelings about you communicating with him. Again, don't let Jared use you to make Cecelia jealous - you're worth MORE than that too!! If you have any other questions don't hesitate to contact me. You should really give Cecelia a call, it might make her feel better about the situation and you'll definitely get the TRUTH from her. Cecelia's a very good person........she would be very civil. I don't want to pressure you the choice is yours. I'm glad you had a great vacation! :)

PSYCHO EX: Hi Karen,

Did you ever find that link with those court case numbers? I hadn't heard back from you. I saw that you just had a b-day...so Happy Belated Birthday hope it was a great one!!! How was the visit with your family?
Well, I haven't heard back from you and I just wanted to make sure I hadn't offended you in anyway. I really do mean well by disclosing this info to you. I know that Jared and Cecelia are still involved. Does he still call you? Well I don't mean to pry but I really think Cecelia should know. Hope you have a great week.

ME (THE DISMISSAL): Melissa,

This has been a very weird situation and I am exiting it. The bombardment of emails, many calls on the Private Number, and messages has actually been a bit of a damper on my vacation. This answers the how was your vacation question. After repeated pleas from Cecelia to call her - which costs money from Canada that I am not willing to spend talking to a stranger - maybe you can relay a message to her.

I AM NOT INTERESTED IN JARED. I have written to him and told him that this situation is bizarre and I want nothing to do with it. All I will say is that I have not even met Jared in person! If he told her anything else, it is simply not true. Cecelia's info about that we had talked to each other at different times during the day is correct, but at this point, he could be the greatest guy in the world and I want NOTHING TO DO WITH HIM -

```
With all the things that were said about him, it is odd she
obviously still wants to be with him so much, but that is
none of my business. It doesn't matter to me. It also seems
that if the point was to "warn me off" of a potentially
dangerous guy, that one or at the most two messages (phone or
otherwise) would have sufficed. This will be my last email.
Please relay this information to your friend so I can be done
with the whole situation.
```

These many emails created a picture of Jared that bore no resemblance to the person whom I had been relating over the phone. But realistically speaking, what did I really know about this guy? There were allegations that Jared was still sleeping with "Psycho" and that he was manipulative, controlling and often targeted "attractive, well-educated, and kind women." These messages were a strange combination of "run for it, Jared is a nut job, with the sentiment that he is the father of my friend's children and they are trying to make it work… but don't forget, he raped her and was abusive."

In response, I wrote back to "Melissa", who I now believe was the ex, herself, and told her I was not romantically involved with Jared. This had fueled several new emails, each one containing schizophrenically different sub messages. As you have read in the above messages, at one moment this completely unknown figure was wishing me a belated happy birthday and hoping I had enjoyed my holidays, and at the next, making me feel that if I communicated with Jared at all, I was a home wrecker.

Deciding to deal with the situation when I returned to Canada, so my trip in the Dominican Republic would not be ruined, I didn't check my phone messages until the plane was taxiing down the Vancouver runway. Not one, but three, messages awaited me from Psycho. The absurdity and surreal stream of chatter that invaded my puzzled mind, was disturbing and odd. Now I was starting to think that I needed to buy myself some supplies - a wig in every hair color, big sunglasses, and possibly enter a witness protection program.

It is only a matter of time before she finds me, I thought. Memories of those really creepy Lifetime movies started to flicker in my mind, and that was when I knew that no matter what happened I needed to flee from this situation. I could almost imagine the sinister score of music playing in the background. At this point in the movie you would tell the seemingly clueless protagonist to get out and run for her life. The revelation I experienced was that even if Jared were the only man left in the Western Hemisphere, dealing with kids and an insane lunatic would still create too many insurmountable difficulties with which I was not remotely prepared to deal. So after receiving a few more emails, I wrote the necessary blow-off email to Jared, explaining that this scenario was more than I had bargained for.

What made this easier to do was that when I had explained the entire scenario to my friend José, he asked me how the ex had acquired my number. When I explained it was the 12 year old son who gave it to her, he proclaimed, "Bull*#*t!" After running through what he thought supposedly happened, he declared with certainty, "He is still sleeping with his ex, and when he was in the shower she went through his phone." Even if that were not true, it sure made my fingers fly over the keys when composing my farewell email! And cue final curtain! :

ME: Jared, Two weeks ago I wasn't being bombarded with messages on networking sites, private phone calls, and phone messages. When I talked to you on the phone for hours, I did not plan on having strangers contacting me repeatedly.
Obviously this would not be something that would go away - I can see that after weeks. Sorry-
I wish you the best

JARED: Karen, As I mentioned to you before, you are not the first person she has done this to. She has done this to my collage friends and co-workers. Plus, it makes thing very embarrassing and difficult for me and my kids. Last night my ex said that she talked to you. She admitted that she planned this whole scheme of hers, and apologized to me to bothering you. Unfortunately, I have had enough of this crap. I am taking action on this, so I can get on with my life, and so that this does not happen again. Trust me this will go away immediately! Again, on behalf on myself I apologize for the headaches.

ME (LAST EMAIL): Hey Jared, Things here have been really good - I have to be honest and say that I have received lots of strange messages and calls from people I don't know in regards to you - and have never been put in that type of position before. The predicament I am put in is that even if one of it is true, there are an ex or old friends, or whatever, that dislike you enough to tell me all these horrible things - which in itself is more than a bit daunting. The fact that you are far away and we don't know each other well - I am not sure that I want to end up in a Lifetime movie gone bad with strange people I don't know messaging and calling me. It is too bad - I really enjoyed talking to you. I wish you the best...

Last Email From Jared: What....who are these people? Are you still being bothered? What are they saying? I don't know who these people are? All I can say is never believe someone else's words...I thought you were a different person.

Plus, remember one thing that if someone is trying so hard to say negative things about somebody, then things are mostly likely fiction. I never did anything to you....so I have no worries....good luck!

Or so I thought. When I finally arrived home to El Paso at the end of the summer, I collected my mail, and included with all the bills, invitations, and letters, was a large white envelope. No return address written in the upper left hand corner seemed odd, and I was completely unprepared for what the contents would reveal. The crazy ex had somehow found my address online, and had sent me copies of the domestic assault reports that she had ranted on about in her multiple voice messages to me. The documents were obviously photocopied, but did appear to be official. I had already told Jared that I wasn't interested, but I guess that this disturbed young lady needed to ensure that I would no longer be invading her territory. I wondered what had made this guy such a prize that she would've even wanted him? Especially if all she was accusing him of was true!

Ladies and gentlemen. The show had wrapped. A drama of epic proportions! I cannot stress enough that if you find yourself being brought into a mess that resembles anything like what I went through, make a break for it! It doesn't even matter if he is a nice guy stuck with a crazy ex. If they have children, you will never be able to escape her. They are tied together for life as they will share parenting responsibilities. Throw in the towel. You *will not* come out ahead in this situation!

.... ;-)

The Cowboy and the City Slicker

> After all, he was 27, lived about two hours away, and talked about his adventures in "rodeoing" and working on a ranch. I don't even use ranch dressing on my salad. What in the world did he think we had in common?

In this scenario, I almost don't feel like I have to change the name of this very gallant and kind cowboy, as I feel like he would never crack open this book, but would rather spend his time riding the range or bailing hay.

One morning during my summer vacation, I arose at the crack of 8:30am, and discovered that I'd received a very complimentary email from a young man named B.W. Between the name and the main profile shot on Match.com, I could see I was dealing with a real live cowboy! Yippee-kye-yay!

This was unchartered territory; even entertaining the idea of going out with a guy who had initials as his name. I was willing to bet money that he frequently spouted off phrases such as "I reckon I should" or "y'all fixin' to ride that stallion now?" Is there anything more manly or sexy than a sweaty man dismounting from a horse?

It would be impossible to lie and say that I was not at all intrigued. After all, he was 27, lived about two hours away, and talked about his adventures in "rodeoing" and working on a ranch. I don't even use ranch dressing on my salad. What in the world did he think we had in common? With nervous trepidation, I opened the email. I could almost hear the Texan accent through the screen, but the text was so complimentary that he immediately had me "roped in". Sorry, but I have to include some of these puns, though I do want to inform you that I have also shown a lot of unseen restraint thus far.

Anyway, B.W. was not a man of many words, but the ones he used were praising my smile, looks, and profile info. I also found out that his beliefs in God appeared to be similar to mine, which finally answered the question as to what we had in common. Now my inquiry to that was - would that be enough to offset the astronomical and obvious differences in our lifestyles? It was less than 24 hours later that I happened to check my mail and received an instant message from said cowboy. There was a problem with this feature functioning properly, so our conversation was a bit stilted and frustrating. The highlight and memorable detail was that he'd asked me if I wanted free tickets to the rodeo to watch him ride in the fall. Never in my life had I been to a rodeo, and I was definitely curious. Even if we didn't get along, I liked trying new things, especially new things that involved rugged, tough, and mildly sweaty men.

During the few phone calls that we shared before the rodeo came to town, I found B.W. to be charming, self-depreciating, and surprisingly intelligent. Knowing that I would not want to attend a rodeo without proper backup, I invited my friend Colleen. She loves this scene, and was over the moon that she would be present for my first real cowboy gathering. Figuring that we would go big or go home, we decked ourselves out in blue jeans, black t-shirts, and cowgirl hats!

It was important for us to meet up with B.W. before the event, otherwise we would not have been able to get in for free and sit in the VIP section, where you could practically smell the cow manure. Via cell phone, we coordinated a meeting place, and my first impression was that he was humble and down-to-earth. Unfortunately, he was not especially my type looks wise. This meant that he was Colleen's type, as we have completely different tastes in men. Perhaps this had worked out for the best, as they were closer in age. I was not particularly disappointed, but more excited to see the bucking broncos and other events.

About halfway through the rodeo, the winds were kicking up to almost torrential speeds. You could feel the air become thicker, and Colleen and I quickly decided to make a sprint for the shelter at the top of the bleachers. We managed this in the nick of time, because seconds later, the rain beat down like an angry bully looking for another victim. Then the rain transformed into pebbles of hail. Those who hadn't foreseen this disastrous turn of events were drenched to the bone, not to mention bruised! Thinking the rodeo was over; Colleen and I were ready to leave.

Stuck in the crowd with nowhere to go, we finally got a call from B.W. telling us that the rain had lessened to a mere drizzle. The plan was that the rodeo would go on!

Seriously?! Wasn't the location of the events a mud pit at this point? That couldn't be safe. This cowboy culture was obviously hard-core! Even though I was impressed, part of me wondered how dangerous this could get. From a distance, all the cowboys looked alike to me. The only distinguishing feature that B.W. had was his entry number. He managed to stay on the bucking bronco for several seconds, and the crowd cheered for him.

Soon after this event, the hoopla was over. Everything was being packed up, so Colleen and I waited for a call from B.W. to see what we might do next. When I casually mentioned we should go to Starbucks for coffee with him and his friend, Colleen openly laughed at me. "Karen, real cowboys don't go to Starbucks. That is way too frou-frou for them, with all the foam, syrups, and bells and whistles." Apparently cowboys liked their coffee the way I liked my men - hot and strong (Sorry I couldn't resist).

Sure enough, when the arrangements were made, Denny's became the cowboys' desired location for our meeting. Good thing Colleen was there to make sure I didn't make a fool of myself, being the "high maintenance" city slicker I truly am.

When we arrived, B.W. and his friend were sitting by the window, still decked out in all their rugged cowboy gear. I don't remember his buddy's name, but he was a very attractive guy. That was until he started talking. Don't ask me how we arrived at the topic of diversity, but that was when the nameless one suddenly stated, "The first time I saw a black person was in college." Colleen and I just stared blankly at him for a moment. Ok, so maybe he had been raised in a primarily Caucasian area of Texas, but we weren't sure what the point of that remark was supposed to have been.

This is where any chance that B.W. had with me went out the window. Mysteriously, the topic had shifted to politics. This date took place right around the time Barak Obama was running for president. It was obvious that the cowboy duo were not in favor of having an African American president, and Colleen and I were challenging their views. B.W. finally declared, without shame, "Obama is my favorite >>>>>>", finishing his sentence with the horrifically offensive "N" word! In disbelief, my jaw hit the ground, and both Colleen and I were momentarily stunned to silence. Picking up that he had obviously not only crossed, but leapt over the line of what was socially/morally appropriate, B.W. tried to pass the comment off as a joke. We were NOT laughing. Needless to say, the dinner was pretty much over.

Less than 5 minutes after we had parted ways, B.W. called and started talking to me like nothing was wrong. In fact, he was trying to set up the next time we could hang out. Avoiding any type of commitment to a future meeting, it still took him awhile to figure out I wasn't interested. I could deal with wearing chaps as if they are legitimate articles of clothing, I could deal with the smell of manure at the rodeo events, and I could even deal with the country music. What I could not stomach was the racism. This was something that I could not overlook. Whether he was joking or not, we all know that out of the heart, the mouth speaks.

.... ;-)

Blake: the English Gentleman

Let me just interject that I do not feel there is anything sexier than a British accent. My theory is that these men sound so distinguished and intelligent, that it automatically makes them more attractive.

Pen pals since the days when I first learned that IM stood for instant message, Blake and I met on a dating site and hit it off immediately. He was one of those stereotypically tall, dark and handsome men. Down to earth and easy to talk to, we struck up a very comfortable cyber-friendship. Obviously from the get go, we knew that it was unlikely that we would ever meet. Blake was from England. An ocean separated us, and as much potential as we could see, we obviously lived in two different worlds, not to mention, on two different continents.

We would run into each other on MSN messenger and chat whenever we had the chance. Over the years we never discussed dating or the potential for romance. There was occasional flirting, but nothing overt.

Approximately nine years after we'd first "met", Blake found me on Facebook, and sent me a friend request. It had been awhile since we had instant messaged, as I had been teaching and was never online during the day (early evening in England). After eagerly accepting his request, we sent some messages back and forth. I would not be obnoxious and dare to declare that he was interested. Yet, he had looked me up, and he had begun to pour his heart out to me. He had told me about his spiritual struggles, work issues, and I had reciprocated. At some point one of us, and I can't actually remember who, made the comment that even though we had been in sporadic contact for over a decade, that we had never even heard each others' voices.

Fast forward to a week later when I was on lunch break and walking down to the teacher's lounge to heat up my meal. My cell phone started belting out my overbearing ringtone, and as I checked the caller ID, I noticed the number began with 011. Being that I had become accustomed to traveling frequently, I recognized this as being an international call.

Baffled and bewildered, I answered.

"Helllllllllllo, Karen?" I was immediately struck by the blatant British accent. Let me just interject that I do not feel there is anything sexier than a British accent. My theory is that these men sound so distinguished and intelligent, that it automatically makes them more attractive. Obviously, it was Blake!

He had asked for my phone number on Facebook, but it had been so long before that I had forgotten.

Just as we began our conversation, my unreliable Sprint Blackberry decided to drop the call. A minute later he called me back, and we talked for a few very expensive minutes. As great as this brief interchange was, it only solidified what we both already knew. He may have had a great accent and been a Christian, but the bottom line was that the distance factor was insurmountable, and we both knew it. Overseas men, even the quality ones, should not be considered viable options unless an opportunity to meet is imminent. How would you get to know each other? Do not get drawn into this distracting situation, which can result in missed opportunities to date locally.

.... ;=)

Ron: First my Boyfriend and Then my Boss

> We still feel a pang of guilt knowing we sold hundreds of dollars worth of fireworks to townspeople who likely were spending more money on "black cats" and "mini missiles" than they would on their grocery budget for the rest of the month. Not to mention that some of those individuals desperately needed to invest in a competent dentist, with extensive experience in tooth replacement.

For those skeptics who believe that signing up for dating sites is a frivolous waste of money, I would beg to argue that in the case of meeting Ron, it was an unintentionally lucrative venture. It all started with the typical back and forth emails and phone calls. Due to the fact that he lived in Illinois, we spoke on the phone regularly, and waited for the opportune time when he could come visit me. What I especially admired about him was that he was taking care of his elderly mom, which spoke volumes about his commitment to family, and his moral integrity.

Eventually one April, Ron made the road trip from southern Illinois to El Paso, Texas, with one of his friends. He was absolutely adorable, and was just as attractive in person as in his picture! We had clicked immediately, and he genuinely seemed to be interested in getting to know me better. To remove all doubt from my mind, he asked me on the last day of his trip if I would be his girlfriend. Even though it seemed premature, I went ahead and accepted. He mentioned that he might need help selling fireworks at his stand in July, and offered me the job. As a missionary, I knew the extra money would not go to waste, so I agreed.

Long story short. I went. When I laid eyes on the town with a population of 200, and realized that there was not a Barnes and Noble or Starbucks within spitting distance (or at least a 20 mile radius), I felt as displaced as a shark in a swimming pool. Immediately I suspected the relationship did not stand a chance. If anyone would have asked me if I'd considered myself to be a city girl, I would have answered with an emphatic, "No!" Yet, when push came to shove, I knew I needed more than one blinking traffic light, gas station coffee, and an overpriced general store to function.

Of course I am leaving out the fact that Ron and I were also not a good romantic match, but luckily we ended up being fantastic coworkers!

On my first visit there, what was meant to be a romance/work combination, turned out to be a work-dominated friendship. When out at the fireworks stand, Ron would become so preoccupied with selling (in his defense, he had invested a lot into the product), that I would often go without food or water for extended periods of time. It wasn't his fault, as I believe that it had been a long time since he had needed to think about the needs of a significant other, and was just rusty at having to cater to a woman's wishes. If I was lucky, I was able to strong arm him into releasing me for 20 minutes, so I could walk over to the Dairy Queen to buy a drink and enjoy the air conditioner. By the end of the week, he felt more like a brother than a beau.

Even though the little town, where the fireworks stand was set up, was a raging Mecca compared to where Ron lived, it still lacked any type of draw for me. We sold fireworks from dawn to dusk every day, and made a killing! As a result, Ron compensated me very generously! I even decided to buy his sporty, blue, Honda CRX from him, and was able to return to El Paso in a new (to me) car! Even though we didn't last as a couple, we've actually maintained a true friendship.

For many summers afterward, I continued selling fireworks with Ron. To this day, we still laugh about the unsavory clientele with whom we did business. We still feel a pang of guilt knowing we sold hundreds of dollars worth of fireworks to townspeople who likely were spending more money on "black cats" and "mini missiles" than they would on their grocery budget for the rest of the month. Not to mention that some of those individuals desperately needed to invest in a competent dentist, with extensive experience in tooth replacement.

Not only did Ron and I make good business associates, but if you go to Shelbyville, Illinois, you can look me up in the newspaper archives. (I'm kind of a big deal there). They did an interview with me about the fireworks stand. Being the patriot I am, I threw in the part about how I was Canadian in order to drum up more interest. Maybe that is what pushed me all the way to a front page piece, complete with a respectable sized photo. Before my head gets too big, it could be argued that the newspaper "journalist" had already interviewed all of the local townspeople, and I was the only person left to speak with!

For those who feel that online dating is just sucking the money out of your wallet and has no value, I think I have just proven to you that it can be lucrative, both financially and personally. A new friend was made, I had the opportunity to legitimately experience the simple country life, and I made several thousand dollars, which supplemented my missionary income each year that I made my trek.

.... ;=)

Doug: Should I Stay or Should I Go?

Anything is possible, but at the rate our romantic relationship is moving forward, we will likely have our rehearsal dinner at a restaurant with early bird specials, where we can receive a sizeable senior citizen's discount!

Back in the early years of venturing online to find love, I met Doug on a Christian website. The profile picture he had posted made him look like a model. This man was unlike many men I had encountered before, and possessed unique traits and life experiences that fascinated me.

First of all, Doug is Korean-American, but was adopted and raised by white parents in Michigan. He was also hip, trendy, and very conflicted as to what he wanted to do with his future. We would chat a lot online via instant messenger, and he was extremely flirtatious and complimentary. As much as I enjoyed the conversations we would have, he lived in Ohio, one of the few states in the US I had not yet managed to visit! I had never had a reason to go there, so I assumed that nothing would ever come of our casual connection.

Then one spring day, Doug asked me if I thought it might be a good idea for him to come on staff for one of our youth missions trips during the summer. I had already been planning to go on the trip, and after talking to the director, I encouraged him to apply. As women, don't we wish we could make *all* potential suitors go through an application process?

Not only did Doug have to provide a lot of detailed answers that revealed his world views and faith, he also had to provide references from his pastor, employer, and friends. As I was a part of the local team staff, I needed to be part of the decision making process as to whether we accepted him or not. This required me reading all of those answers and forms.

There was something a little disconcerting about knowing so much about someone that I'd never met, and who I may have ended up potentially dating. Then add to the mix that if he joined the team, we were going to work together closely for an entire month, in an environment where romantic relationships were clearly frowned upon, while chaperoning 20 teenagers.

After his application for staff leader had been scrutinized, Doug was accepted for the position, and for almost four weeks we worked together 24-7 on the outreach. I definitely felt this equaled about 6 months of regular "weekend" dating relationships, because I saw Doug deal with unusual, and sometimes difficult, situations that were unexpectedly thrown at him.

Before we knew it the mission trip was over. Our team had passed through our survival wilderness adventure and outreach without any trouble. The point of having the teens rough it in the woods was to help them toughen up in time to take them on outreach, where living conditions were often more difficult than what they were used to. Also there was the added bonus that leadership qualities were fostered, and team cooperation naturally occurred. You know what else occurred? Doug having the opportunity to see me sweaty, going without a shower for three days, wearing no makeup (except for a little eyeliner contraband that I managed to sneak in), and being dog-tired from lack of sleep.

Later, he admitted to me that he'd thought I'd looked really hot in my hiking shorts, and that is why he'd always stayed behind me on the trail! What does one say to that? Throughout the trip, Doug saw me at my best and my worst. That would make it almost the perfect "non-dating" dating relationship. He saw me mentoring kids. He saw me trying to serve others and work hard. He saw me sweaty and dirty. The pressure was off since we knew that this trip would not be the time to start a romantic relationship, so with that off the table we were able to become friends. There were times when I wasn't sure if I was interested, and then times where Doug seemed almost irresistible to me.

When the trip was over, Doug had one more day to hang out before he had to fly home. It was a treat to be able to spend time together without the watchful eyes of our team members peering over at us. He offered to cook me dinner, and since he was so charming, I was starting to wonder if he was about to take things to a more romantic place.

When the dinner was ready and the mood was set, we were interrupted by a few of the teen boys who had been on the trip with us. They pretty much invited themselves over for dinner, and even though Doug hesitantly agreed, it was obvious that he did not want to share my attention with these youngsters. After dinner, the boys conveniently left, or so we thought.

When asked what he wanted to do for his last night in El Paso, Doug's choice had been to watch a movie with me. A romantic comedy, if I remember correctly. Sitting on the loveseat, with the lights lowered, we started the show. That was when every twenty minutes or so, my young male fan club from dinner would tap on the windows or knock on the door. They'd explained to me later that they had known exactly what Doug's intentions were with me, and they were bound and determined to stop the budding flirtation! Well, it worked. We never kissed, and the next morning I dropped Doug off at the airport, where he made no promises of us getting together again or starting a romantic relationship.

Every six months or so, Doug resurfaces to flirt with me. He would tell me how he wishes he had kissed me and not let the teen boys scare him off that night. He mentions how he fondly remembers me as being sexy and sweet at the same time. He assures me that one day he thinks we may end up together, and that God had us meet for a reason. From Ohio, and then from Korea, he has randomly contacted me and professed his adoration.

Over seven years later I am still in this "on hold" mode with Doug. If he can get a job in El Paso, if he moves back from Korea, if we can somehow end up in the same place to start dating - then it might work out. Who knows? Anything is possible, but at the rate our romantic relationship is moving forward, we will likely have our rehearsal dinner at a restaurant with early bird specials, where we can receive a sizeable senior citizen's discount!

.... ;-)

Josh: Mr. Desperate McClingy

Here is where I have to interject that I tend to almost act like a man in a relationship sometimes. Being super independent, I often feel that I require less maintenance than a lot of other women do. In fact, I often feel that I require a lot less maintenance then a lot of men do.

If you end up looking for love online long enough, you will certainly meet a Josh on your journey! This story almost did not make it into this book. With a deadline looming, this vignette desperately needed further editing if it was going to be added. Josh's chapter was about to land on the "cutting room floor", I decided that this account could be tremendously helpful to many women (and men), out there.

I met Josh on a Christian dating site, hoping that a love connection would blossom. I recall that he sent me a picture that was attractive, where he was decked out in stylish sunglasses and a polo shirt. The problem was that this image ended up being deceptively cute - once I saw an actual photo where he had taken off the sunglasses, his entire look changed! His eyes were sunken in and dull. He appeared a lot older, and what can I say, he just wasn't my type! Physical attraction is important, and I was seriously reconsidering the idea of trying to create a long distance relationship with someone that I was not "feeling it for."

Here is where I have to interject that I tend to almost act like a man in a relationship sometimes. Being super independent, I often feel that I require less maintenance than a lot of other women do. In fact, I often feel that I require a lot less maintenance then a lot of _men_ do. In El Paso, some women I have run into seem to possess that "needy vibe" that I cannot stomach. I do not need my boyfriend to drop me off and then call me when he gets home. I do not need to be constantly calling or texting back and forth. If anything, this excessive type of attention and communication begin to interfere in my everyday life activities, and is guaranteed to create a sense of resentment in me.

When Josh first asked me for my phone number, I never dreamed that he would be texting me late at night, at ungodly hours in the morning on weekends (gasp - before 8am), and that he would spout off sweet talk that would have suggested that we had already embarked on the relationship train. It might be understandable that Josh probably viewed me as a catch and was staking his territory, but it was too much, too soon, and too intense in every way. I started purposefully leaving my phone in the car, at home, anywhere that I could escape the bombardment of "Hey girl!" texts and "Hope you are doing great, call me as soon as you get this" phone messages.

The situation began to feel like someone had grabbed a gigantic fluffy pillow and was headed my way. Everyone likes a fluffy pillow right? Not when they are about to use it to smother the last living breath out of you! And that was how I felt; like Josh was going to suffocate me with his constant need for attention and affirmation. The never ending reassurance that I was required to shower upon him was exhausting! I was feeling like a mouse trapped in the corner, with the safety of my hole in the wall just inches out of reach.

Make me run on the treadmill for an hour! Make me stay up all night and go to work the next day! Make me logically reason with 4 year olds. Make me do anything, rather than succumb to having this guy slowly suck the life out of me! Dramatic right?

As I suffered through a few weeks of this, suddenly a light flashed on in my head, and I realized that I was not officially dating this man. I had not even met him in person yet. No promises had been stated, yet in the end I felt like I had to "break up with him"; even as he was clutching onto me, or the idea of who he thought I was, for dear life. I had to pry his fingers, one by one, to release me from the emotional death grip he had me trapped in. As you can see from the email below, I ended up terminating communication with Josh via email:

Hey Josh,

I am trying to think of how to write this email, because I am not quite sure how to do it - I think this morning for me solidified the fact that I needed to, and you have said that honesty and communication are important to you, so here it goes...

The amount of calling and texting has become overwhelming for me, and for where we are in how well we know each other, it seems excessive. Even my best friends and I do not text and call so often, and I find it distracting sometimes from what I am doing or working on. This morning was my only day to sleep until 8am - and I have told you before that I use my phone as an alarm. Not only did you text me so early, but followed that up with a phone call - It was very frustrating for me not to be able to get back to sleep, but still be tired, as I was up late last night. When I finally did get back to sleep, I missed getting up in time to go to church, which was a bummer for me.

I think there are a lot of girls out there that would appreciate a guy that would show them so much attention via texts and phone calls. In fact a lot of girls I know in El Paso require that of the guys they date, but I guess that I

am just not as receptive to that. I tried to tell you once on
the phone about this, via the checking in comment, but I
don't know if that really got the message across.

At this point I am not sure what to do, because you mentioned
that communication is one of the most important things to you
- It is to me too, but not the frequency that I think you
like. You are very nice Josh, and I am sure that you are a
great guy. I just don't know if we are going to be compatible
in this way. I wrote this in an email because it is hard to
say to someone that you want less communication without
making them feel bad, and I hate that. Yet I have to be
honest.

Maybe we can take a break from communicating for a bit, and
see how it goes? I know I am going to be really busy today
and until I finish grading those essays - I also understand
if you decide to look elsewhere for a relationship that meets
more of your communication needs after reading this email. It
has been nice to meet you though, and I did enjoy talking to
you.

Some of you may think that I was heartless to "break up" with him in such an impersonal way, and to you I declare: "We were NOT even dating, so I did not break up with him. I merely decided to move on, and at least I informed him. A lot of people decide to quit all cyber communication without any kind of explanation. Feel free to use any portion of the above email to express yourself if you should have the misfortune of finding yourself in my situation! Discussing how I felt with Josh would have been a useless endeavor, and I did not wish to engage in a verbal sparring match with him. From the email below, it was evident that I had made the right choice in not speaking with him; he had a lot of arguments which were coming at me from all directions! Also, not to be a spelling snob, but if this email was supposed to have been an insightful and persuasive means to keep me interested, he should have at least proofread it before sending it:

CYBERWINK

> Karen, I guess I'll say few things! I don't understand why you would write this long e-mail when you could just call and talk to me and let me know how you feel. I would respect the fact for you. I'm a big boy and a tough 31 year old guy who is very independent and loves life. You won't hurt my feelings by you explaining your feelings to me about what's on your mind. That I can except and how you feel about us talking and texting TWICE a day the last week. If I remember we talked about this and you mention it didn't bother you. OK................SO i messed up once and I'm human. I made a mistake. Last night you texted me to call in the am. You never told or mention what time exactly to call. So how was I suppose to know. My texts to you aren't asking for a response back. They are more like you are a "awesome person you", "You have a good day", and " hope your day is going well".....so on.
>
> I hope this helps. I don't know I use to be the guy that never reached out before. But my friends and family have said that some of my problem to a relationship was not reaching out. So I start doing it to you and I get in trouble. I even tried very hard when my cousin was here last weekend to take time and to make it a point to talk to you. I enjoyed so much listening to you and getting to know you. I don't even know why this is even a issue. This is starting to just be drama.
>
> Just call me. I'll guess I will take a break. I really not interested looking else where unless your not interested anymore. I understand. Sorry reaching out to much.

If along your internet dating path you run into a suction cup cling-on as I did, be sure to detach yourself as soon as possible. Try not to feel too sorry for Josh, because if I remember correctly, he ended up dating another girl fairly quickly afterwards (which I knew from a change in his social networking profile to "in a relationship"). This type of man is not one to stay single long, but will quickly scour the prospects and find another human being to connect to.

Tips for the Woman Who Is Serious about Online dating

1. You absolutely must have appropriate photos on your profile.

IN FACT, YOU SHOULD have at least two or three pictures. As it is, a majority of guys are likely to ask you for more photos, especially ones that show that you are not fat, you have all your teeth, and do not have a lazy eye. Resist the urge to put up a picture that shows a lot of skin. You do want to be thought of as a girl who can be taken home to Mom, not just a girl who can be taken home, don't you?

Do not use overly posed pictures. (Ladies, this means no Glamour Shots!). This makes it look like you are trying too hard. You will run across many men who take these kinds of shots, sometimes focusing on their abs. Is this a fellow who wants to settle down, or is this a man who is brazenly seeking as many women to touch those abs as possible? (This was written before the days of the MTV reality show "Jersey Shore" that showcases "The Situation" and his infamous 6 pack).

Make sure that one of your profile photos is a close up, without sunglasses. Contrary to what we, as women, would think, many men are actually attracted to pretty eyes and a great smile. It is a mistake to put up pictures of yourself that are really outdated and look more like your younger sister than you.

We would not want this scam pulled on us (and believe me, it has happened to me and I was NOT happy). In fact, try to cut out any pictures that are over 2 years old, just to be safe. This is also a way to protect you from getting hurt, as the guy has a realistic idea of your look, and will not be bitterly disappointed when he first lays eyes on you. Men are visual creatures. Why would you want to invest any time or energy into communicating with someone who may just dismiss you in the end as he felt you were dishonest with him, because of the archaic photos you posted?

Delete all those group pictures with friends who are more attractive than you are, as the superficial guys will potentially ask you if your friends are single, and try to score their email addresses. This could be an effective way of weeding out some of the losers, but it may come at the expense of your ego or self-esteem! A reliable gauge I use when considering a photo for an online profile is that it makes you look approachable, interesting, and at your best.

I remember a time when I was texting a young man, but had not had the opportunity to meet him in person. After a late karaoke session, I had received a text from him asking if I had gone out that night. Turns out he had been at the same place, and had recognized me from my online pictures! He must have thought I was cute enough to consider as dating potential, because he did proceed to ask me out.

Declining his offer was my response, as a combination of a very busy schedule, being apprehensive about his age (25 years), and realizing that he had not had the confidence to approach when he was fairly sure that it was me. After this exchange, I simply felt a meeting would be a waste of time for both of us. At least I learned from that experience that I was not misrepresenting myself (he'd had no idea I was even going out that evening).

Also, if you are on the fence about posting your possible profile photos, enlist a trustworthy friend; preferably a guy friend. The platonic male pals I have, the ones not looking to hook up with me, have always been brutally honest about which pictures were flattering or unflattering. These men are the most reliable and unfailing resources you have!

2. No photo on his profile? Proceed With Caution!

There will be times when you will receive emails from men who have no photos posted on their profile. I have found that there are three main reasons for this being the case.

Perhaps these men are quite unattractive, and do not believe that women would respond to them if they immediately saw what they looked like. Also, some are just shy about having their photos on the web for all to see. They think that perhaps coworkers may run across their pictures, or they might be uncomfortable joining a matchmaking site because they feel it is embarrassing to meet someone online instead of naturally.

The third reason, and I believe the most dishonorable one, is that they are either married or have girlfriends. These guys are just looking to flirt or possibly cheat, with different women, and do not want to be discovered. There may possibly be other reasons, but those are the common three that I have encountered.

When these men shoot you an email, ask them immediately if they have photos that they can send, so you can put a face to the person. They should be willing to do this, and if they are not, consider that to be a waving red flag of warning. Don't feel that you are being shallow by asking to see what they look like. You are on a DATING site. It should be a reasonable assumption that you would need to discover if there is any potential physical chemistry. Hopefully you will take the time to hand pick the pictures you post, and your suitor will have the advantage of seeing those. It is only fair that they would be willing to return the favor.

3. Actually read the guy's profile.

A boyish smile and twinkling blue eyes may seem to jump through the screen at you, but if this man only listens to gangster rap, has 10 cats, and lists his mother as his best friend, you might want to consider compatibility as a factor. Does he share your same beliefs? Is he looking for someone who wants to have 5 kids? No kids? Does he have a job? Note, that in order to decide what is important to you in the profile, you should have already determined and decided your non-negotiable and deal-breaking criteria ahead of time.

Also, you may find that there is something about you that he has already stated in his profile for which he is specifically looking or NOT looking. Trust me when I say it is embarrassing to get a reply from a man that says, "Didn't you read in my profile that I am limiting my search to women in my area?!" or "I only want to date women younger than 30 years old." Some men are very particular, and they are entitled to their preferences, just as you are.

Let's be honest. If your idea of camping is staying in the Marriot on the outskirts of a city, do you really want to end up with a guy who stated in his profile that his idea of the perfect weekend getaway is extreme camping and deep sea fishing? Do you see yourself digging a latrine? Using leaves as toilet paper?

Remember that as a woman in pursuit of a possible love connection, these guys ought to sell themselves to you, and not just sit in judgment of whether you will be right for them or not. As one chasing down love, you will be tempted to conveniently "overlook" some of the information that does not necessarily appeal to you. Instead of doing this, address any of these concerns as tactfully as you can in the first few emails, to measure whether you want to continue to invest any more time conversing with that particular individual.

4. <u>Do a detailed search for prospective guys of interest on your matchmaking site.</u>

Any online dating site worth its membership fee should have a feature where you can do a customized search. This is genius if you hold tightly onto those "deal breakers" on which you know you cannot, under any circumstances, compromise. For example, if you know that your potential boyfriend has to be taller than you, has to be a non-smoker, has to have never been married, or has to want children, you can narrow down the number of profiles to read through using this customized search mechanism.

Be careful not to be so picky about superficial characteristics that you eliminate a prospective soul mate. Sometimes we may not know what we actually need, and perhaps that is the reason we may still be single. For me, it is crucial that the man is a Christian, because my faith profoundly affects my world view and how I live my life. Whether he is 5'6" or 6'4" is irrelevant, and speaks nothing of his character or integrity, which, in my opinion, is the real substance of a man.

> 5. Use the various features on the websites that help you initiate and maintain contact.

What do you do with the features on the sites that are there simply for the purpose of showing someone that you are interested? Should you take the bull by the horns and make the first move? Shoot off a "wink"?

To be honest, I think that is the most proactive thing a woman can do. I was telling one of my best friends who is now just giving the online scene a try, that there is no harm in showing a guy on a site that you are curious, and have noticed something special about him. This should be considered a compliment, and remember that men are on these sites because they are single too, and most are probably looking to find a relationship.

I believe that once you have shown interest, a guy will check out your profile and the pictures you have posted first, and then if he thinks there is some potential, he will **promptly** reply to you, and continue the communication. A man, usually in any circumstance, just needs a bit of encouragement in order for him to approach a single woman, if he is attracted to her.

I would often do a customized search, check out the profiles, and then wink at the guys who interested me in some way. As mentioned in a previous tip, make sure you read the men's profiles. Some of them dislike winks, and will not appreciate this gesture, which they see as a lack of effort in writing them a message.

Due to the sheer volume of profiles out there, I suggest sending short personal notes to only the ones in whom you are truly interested. Try to find something in their profiles on which you can specifically comment, and keep it short and light-hearted. Declaring that you believe you could be soul mates, telling him what baby names are your favorites, or giving him an uncensored personal history, are sure turn-offs.

6. If there is a "Who is Online Now" feature, definitely use it.

We are all creatures driven by instant gratification. Thanks to the "Online Now" features on many dating websites, you can mingle through messages or chat effortlessly. A guy who you may not have bothered emailing otherwise, may be someone you end up chatting with for a few minutes, and finding that there is potential. Also, there could be an interesting guy who you missed when doing your search. Try going online at different times of the day to "run" into different types of men. It was exactly this feature that led me to meet my boyfriend, Fernando, who I even envisioned marrying.

In that case, it had been about a month since I had checked one particular dating site, as usually there were not local men who had posted profiles there. After looking to see "Who is Online", I ran across Fernando's profile, and although it had not been filled out completely, it was intriguing. I shot off a quick wink, and before I knew it, he had responded by instant messaging me on the site. He has even told me that the brief chat we'd had at that time was instrumental in sparking his interest.

I firmly believe that if I had not checked him out this way, I wouldn't have even returned to the site for several weeks, and by then he would have been finished with his free trial. As a result, we would never have made the connection that led us to meeting and starting an incredible relationship!

7. Getting personal: Chatting online or texting

After a few emails back and forth, most guys who are serious about trying to get to know you will ask if you can chat with them online sometime. This is where you need to have a commonly used chat, such as Yahoo or MSN, where you can meet. Some sites have the added benefit of an Instant

Messaging feature where you can just chat there, but they are often slow, and may quit on you occasionally. Many times, just having a short dialogue with a guy will reveal if there is any type of connection present, and if your personalities click.

In the last few years, I've learned that many men would rather just skip this step, and may ask for your phone number so that they can text with you. My serious suggestion is to make sure that you have a real feel for the man who asks before you volunteer your digits. On one occasion, I gave my number to a suitor who had emailed me a few times. Afterwards, I discovered that there were some relationship deal breakers with him, and he would not be compatible with me. I let him know, via text message, that going out wasn't an option for us. His response was very aggressive, and even derogatory. A slough of unsavory texts invaded my inbox. Not knowing how to block his phone number, it took weeks of ignoring him before he finally left me alone.

Be patient, and get to know a guy through emails and chat first. If he seems in too much of a hurry to skip this "getting to know you stage", that could be a warning sign. If he still tries to insist that you communicate with phone calls and texts, not understanding your explanation that you don't casually give out your personal phone number to strangers, then I would highly recommend cutting off contact with this disrespectful individual.

Once you feel comfortable that the man is a decent and truthful person, then it is a calculated risk for you to start texting. For me this was helpful in a way, as far as moving things along. There would be exchanges that would quickly show me whether or not this person was one I would be interested to meet in person, and often this has resulted in less time wasted with a week's worth of lengthy emails!

My boyfriend, Fernando, started texting me almost immediately, and I truly believe that it did help us to connect during the day in a relaxed manner, and eventually led to daily phone calls. (There are exceptions to every rule)

Another extreme when attempting to get more personal, is that your man of interest avoids chatting with you, even after you have sent each other numerous emails. This could signify that he is not yet emotionally ready for a relationship, but is toying with the idea. It is possible he could already be in a relationship or even married, and does not feel free to release his contact info. Even though the Internet is obviously an artificial means of getting to know someone, try to let the process flow as naturally as possible.

8. The sites can be addicting, but log off already!

These matchmaking and dating sites can be very time consuming! Now ironically, one of the main reasons that regular, everyday men and women sign up is because they don't have a lot of extra time in their busy lives to go out and meet other singles. For example, I knew that I was not going to meet a potential love interest at work. There were no men my age or who shared important commonalities with me at the school where I was teaching, and although I took pleasure in learning and worshipping at my church, it had a shortage of single Christian men in my age group. The all women's bible study, of which I was a part, was also understandably not where I would meet my dream guy!

You might find yourself in a similar predicament, where you need to utilize the Web to meet eligible bachelors, but I suggest that you assign yourself a certain amount of time per day to check and answer messages, perhaps even prioritizing which guys are the ones you are the most interested in communicating with.

Online websites are as plentiful and varied as you could ever imagine. Some target people of certain races, faiths, or interests; all promising that you will meet Mr. or Miss. Perfect-for-You. If you are new to the online dating scene, it will feel like a whole new world has opened up to you. Instead of having to endure pick-up lines and cheesy come-ons, you get to see an outline of who this person is, what he does for a living, and what his hobbies are. It would take you hours at a club or bar to retrieve all this vital information, not to mention that you will probably not pick up Mr. Relationship in a place like that. These sites are a shopping catalogue filled with men. The greatest part is that you don't have to feel bad if what you discover about an individual makes you cringe. You just delicately exit their profile, and no harm is done. No one's feelings are hurt.

There are some sites that are free to join, and some that require you purchase a membership after a free trial. How can I say this in a tactful way? I believe I will quote my father, "You get what you pay for." Even though I appreciate the concern for my fledgling pocketbook, the quality of guys with profiles on the free sites have always tended to be less than stellar. Possibly true love for them is not worth $39.95?

Many of the men I ran into on these complimentary websites, (remember that I do screen many of the perverts out with my criteria settings) were obviously looking for a fling. It was of no interest to them that I actually wrote the last sentence of my profile stating, "If you are interested in a fling, then you should x out of my profile now." After all, it was obvious that these men were not even reading my profile, just checking out the photos. Since I do not have the typical bikini or cleavage pictures, I am not sure what would lead them to believe that I would be willing to help warm their sheets.

Ultimately, what I am trying to say is that if you don't mind wading through the dregs, go ahead and investigate your options on the no cost venues. You may find the one gold nugget in a sea of fool's gold. I have met a few stand-up gentlemen on the free sites.

Some of the more popular sites out there, such as Match.com, tend to have more of a selection of genuine seekers of romance. At one point, and I hate to admit this, I was sampling several different options at once. (All in the name of research, of course!) Remember that there are websites that cater to different interests and religious preferences, for those who are already aware of what their non-negotiable criteria are! Have fun and experiment with various places, but try not to let the online world take over your life!

At times you will be glued to your screen, or in some cases, your phone (love and hate relationship with technology), waiting for that certain cutie's response. Do you know that you can even purchase a feature which tells you exactly when the object of your interest has read your email? Personally, I don't want that much information!

I may get offended if he doesn't immediately get back to me. Is he writing some other girl right now? What, am I not as important as whoever he must be corresponding with at this very moment? Grab a paper bag and breathe! Likely he did just what you do all the time without realizing it, and read the email right before going out or eating dinner. Don't keep checking the last time your prospect went online, or keep logged on all the time so that others will check you out. That can appear a little desperate and obsessive, rather than passionate.

Keep going out with friends, pursuing your goals, enjoying your hobbies, and growing into the type of person that your future love will find irresistible. Do not overuse dating site features and become a compulsive online detective. Turn off the computer, and go have fun with real live friends and family!

9. You are not the only person with whom he is talking

Do not be offended by the fact that the men you are conversing and flirting with are also conversing and flirting with other women in cyberspace. I guarantee that this will lead to you fixating on when a guy is online, why he is online, and who else besides you he could be connecting with. This will inevitably result in you feeling jealous, insecure, and inadequate.

This happened to me in the early days of my online dating pursuit. The way I'd acted when I had "caught" a man being online, but checking out profiles rather than responding to my last email, was atrocious. It was as if I had already staked my claim on him! As if I were lifting my leg to mark my territory! Then when they'd figuratively "bolted away" from me, I was left feeling wounded and rejected. Don't stress about who someone you're interested in might be talking or emailing with. The question I pose to you is this, "Are you talking to more than one guy?"

Remember that you are likely doing the exact same thing, namely sampling from the smorgasbord of attractive men. You are shopping in the mall of online profiles, seeking that one man who will obviously stand out from all the others. If you can honestly tell me that you are only communicating with one man and forsaking all others, then you likely need to convey the seriousness of your interest to your potential suitor when it's appropriate. If you are like the 99.95% of the online dating website users out there, then it would be more advantageous to look at these dating sites as being a networking tool, where you can meet many different types of people, practice your flirting, and potentially connect with someone special.

Now, what shouldn't you do? Do not make comments about how you saw that he was online, but noticed also that he chose not to write or chat with you at that time. These types of remarks will make him feel as nervous as a long-tailed cat in a room full of rocking chairs. Or they may point toward you being a potential stalker, and he will likely drop you like a hot potato. Be secure in the knowledge that if a relationship is meant to be, you will be the one chosen in the end. Not only that, but you have the right to be choosy yourself. One of the sexiest attributes you can possess to attract a man is bold confidence. Flaunt it!

10. Safety first!

Never agree to meet a stranger in a place where you feel uncomfortable. Make sure that you meet at public, high traffic places, like coffee shops or popular restaurants. Try not to make it the coffee shop that you most often frequent, as that may ruin the place for you, and you end up losing one of your favorite hangouts. Meet your date at the chosen location, and be sure that you let a good friend know where you will be, and who you will encounter there. Remember that as nice as this person might seem, you do not actually KNOW him.

Unlike meeting men naturally through family, coworkers, or friends, there is no one to vouch that this person is who he has claimed himself to be. Here is the tricky part. If you are getting along great with this new guy, he might casually suggest that you go somewhere else after coffee or dinner. No matter how normal he seems, do not go off in his vehicle with him. I repeat, DO NOT DO IT! If he is legitimately a good guy, he will not insist on this. In fact, he will see the wisdom in your actions, and respect your wishes. After all, he probably has a sister, niece, or other important female in his life, and wouldn't recommend that she get in a car with a stranger.

Also, it couldn't hurt to be hesitant when disclosing specific information about where you work, just in case your date ends up being a tad unbalanced and tries to contact you there. Does this sound extreme? It can't hurt to be cautious with a person who is still essentially an "unknown".

11. Mi Casa no es tu Casa.

Even when you have gone out once, wait before revealing where you live. Only you will know when it feels right to give out this information, but it shouldn't be after just one date. Sometimes it takes awhile for someone's true colors to show, and believe me when I say that looks can be deceiving! Have your new suitor meet some of your friends and get their opinions concerning his character. Make sure you give your buddies permission to be honest, without fear of your wrath or defensiveness. Try to remind yourself that they know you and have your best interests at heart.

The only exceptions are guy friends who secretly want to date you (like they are going to give you a thumbs up), or a friend who is jealous and a tad unscrupulous (maybe resents that you are happier than she is).

A worst case scenario would be if you decided you wanted things to end, and the guy came knocking at your door, begging or potentially harassing you. Before you'd know it the police would be arriving, and you'd be on the news! Similar to the idea of not giving your phone number to someone you are not sure you trust, how much more important is it not to give them directions to where you hang your hat! If he is a gentleman, he will, without hesitation, respect your privacy until he has earned your trust.

12. Trust your gut.

If you have a gut feeling that someone is not being truthful with you or is trying to manipulate your feelings, act on that and cut ties with the person in question. There are plenty of guys out there, and your instinct is usually correct. I am not saying to become a Skeptical Sally, always jaded and mistrusting, but the reality is that warning bells do go off for a reason.

We, as women, often want to give a man the benefit of the doubt, and so we dismiss a half-truth, a vague answer to an important question, or a slight put down. We can easily justify shady behaviors with excuses. He didn't really mean to lie to me. I'm sure he would have come around and told me what he was doing. He is a private person. He just doesn't like to talk about his past. He is only shouting and causing drama because he really cares about me.

Automatically dismissing these types of questionable behaviors could lead to an unhappy relationship at best, or a potentially dangerous situation at the worst. Maybe you meet up with a man from a dating website, and you just feel intuitively, as the night progresses, that there is something wrong. Don't be so concerned with being polite that you put yourself in jeopardy. Make up a reason to leave and go. Better to be safe than sorry.

13. Free trials.

Most of the matching sites out there have a standard free trial period. Normally you will not have all the features available to you, as they are trying to reel you in to join by paying for a membership. They hook you by allowing you to check out the various profiles, where you are able to see if there are any interesting prospects in your area. When you spot that guy who is your type, and only you know what type that is, in order for you to be able to send an email to him, you will need to fork out the beyond trial membership cash.

Also, because the sites know that those clients with photos get viewed more often, they will often offer you a longer trial if you upload pictures onto your profile. Sometimes you can get up to a week extra by doing this.

Keep in mind that you can also join dating sites which are completely free, and make their money via advertising. If you remember my mentioning this earlier, I stated that you often "get what you pay for." I would once again emphasize the fact that the men my friends and I have met on these sites, did not appear to be on serious quests for love. (Although there were the odd exceptions) They were clearly on serious quests for a one time hook ups or friends with benefits. Believing that you are most likely reading this because you are looking for a potentially serious relationship, I am not saying it would be impossible to find someone on a free site, but it would definitely be more challenging.

14. Beware of the automatic membership renewals.

I am about to share a tip about matchmaking sites that is going to keep you from becoming so furious that you will want to throw your computer mouse (or even your laptop) across the room. These sites do not exist because they want to make magical connections between two lovebirds. They exist because someone wants to make money. I do not slight the creators as they are providing a service, but once you have given them your credit card information to sign up for a month or longer, many times the site will ***automatically*** renew your membership. This means that they will not inform you when your time has expired, but just charge your credit card again.

I learned this lesson the hard way, and as a result, had to eat peanut butter and jelly sandwiches for the last few days before my paycheck. In order to make sure that this injustice does not happen, you need to check your account settings and make sure that you remove this feature from your account profile, so that it states that when your time is up, that your card will not be used.

On one occasion I had actually gone on several dates with someone, and feeling fairly secure, had planned to let my membership on a major site lapse, but unfortunately got dinged by this annoying feature. When I complained to the customer service department, I was told that this was a service provided as a convenience for the site user. How nice that they felt conveniently entitled to empty my wallet! Don't let this happen to you.

15. Every girl loves a deal.

Just like every girl wants a bargain at the mall, there are bargains to be had with memberships for these dating sites. Seasonal deals are almost always happening, especially around Christmas time. I think that they know that if you are single, this is the tough time of year to be on your own with Christmas, New Years, and Valentine's Day hitting you back to back. All of those family get togethers with your siblings and their spouses, while you fly solo. All of those holiday parties, where you are one of the "singletons".

Let's not even delve into the pressure that any single person feels to have a New Years Eve date, and one he/she actually desires to kiss at midnight! There is something about this time of year that I think has both men and women more open to romance. Often, there are more people joining sites at this time due to the Christmas holidays, when they are free to surf the Web because they have extended breaks from work. Sometimes the New Year also spurs people to prioritize what is really important, and often, they will feel that relationships should rank higher up their lists. It is fantastic that at this prime "hunting season", you may get up to 50% off with these discounted offers, so it really can be a good deal! Keep your eyes open, and pounce when the opportunity presents itself. Dating is hard enough without paying through the nose for the privilege.

16. You can never make another first impression.

Another critical task that you must complete in order to find love online is to make sure that you closely inspect your completed profile once you have answered all the questions. Nothing is worse than when you read over an attractive man's profile and he is telling you what a "grate" person he is! No, I am not an snob because I am an English teacher! Okay, maybe I can be, but I am not the only one out there who will pause when viewing an obvious error. Check for typos, spelling mistakes, and bad grammar. If you do not feel confident about your editing skills, allow a friend or family member to help you, and give their opinions about what you have written. Also, read through and make sure that you have not written anything that may not truly reflect your personality or character.

Maybe you rattle on about how much you love the great outdoors, but the reality is your idea of camping is the occasional picnic in the park. The man who contacts you will likely be hoping to share this hobby with you, and this situation will obviously become a cheesy, slap-stick comedy movie in the making. Ladies, we need to be secure in who we are and not try to present ourselves as who we think men want us to be. If someone is going to fall in love with you, then he needs to have an accurate idea of who you really are as a person, rather than someone who has been fabricated in hopes of attracting men to view your profile.

A sense of humor is critical, and is what will help you stand out from another girl who may just be another pretty face. Also, always keep in mind that if you have been on any particular site for awhile, go back consistently and update any information that may have changed. On one profile I still had it stated that I was working towards my masters degree, when I had completed it **two** years earlier!

17. How far are you really willing to go?

On many of these dating sites there are guys from foreign countries who may contact you. Tread carefully here. I had a guy friend who ended up meeting a girl from South America on a website. After corresponding for awhile, they met up. Quite soon after that, they were engaged and ended up getting married. This was not the fairytale that my friend was hoping for. In fact, it turned out to be a very difficult experience from which he had to untangle himself. Ultimately he had to remove this difficult and complicated woman from his life.

Ask yourself if the "nowhere near" local people writing heartfelt messages are interested in you, or in your ability to provide them with finances, or possibly citizenship if you marry.

Some people desperately want to leave their countries, and see you as a possible vessel to help them escape. Frankly, how well can you get to know a man from Romania via long distance? Consider that even if the person is fantastic, you still may have to deal with near impossible immigration issues and significant cultural differences. These differences might not show up right away, but they will. Regrettably, sometimes infatuation causes people to rush into serious commitments too soon (Yes, I have been guilty of this!).

Even considering someone who lives in another state can be tricky. I dated a guy who was living in California, and after seeing each other 4 times over 5 months, I realized that he had major "deal breaker" issues with which I just could not live. One minute he was picking out the wedding date, and in the next moment he was irrationally accusing me of cheating on him. How much harder to try to pursue a serious romantic relationship with someone thousands of miles away?

18. Watch out for men whose profiles are hidden.

On several occasions I received charming emails from men who seemed sweet and engaging. Then, when I clicked on their user names or pictures, I found that they had "hidden" their profiles. Apparently, it was fine for them to read the profile I'd written, proofed, and generally slaved over, while I was not even allowed a glimpse into theirs? Why are these profiles hidden? Do these gentlemen have something to hide? Every time I have run into this situation, I have called the man out, asking why he would be restricting who might possibly find him.

To this day, I have never heard an answer that could ring true. The old excuses of having coworkers see you online are outdated. Online dating is mainstreamed now, and the shame and stigma once associated with it has dissipated, for the most part. Unless these men are in a federal witness protection program, in which case they shouldn't be dating anyway, there is not a legitimate explanation for why they need to conceal their identities. My belief is that there are females with whom they must be involved in some way (an unsuspecting wife or girlfriend perhaps?). After asking a few male friends about this, they all agreed that hiding a profile seemed underhanded and sly.

After all, if a man is just trying to block some psycho stalker, there are features on most sites that are easy and effortless to operate that will completely resolve this problem. If you must entertain one of these "covert operators", go in with your eyes <u>wide</u> open. Any man who is not being upfront should be held suspect. Consider yourself warned.

19. Don't wait until you've met your cyber beau before enjoying life!

Whatever your passions, whether sports, music, or some other interest, these should be an important part of your life as a single person. When I hear women say, "I want to join a soccer league, but I want to wait to have a boyfriend to go with," or "I really have a desire to buy a home and fix it up, instead of renting, however I want to wait until I get married before taking on that kind of project," I feel like shouting, "Women, it is time to chase your dreams!"

Honestly, what is more attractive than someone who is confident, motivated, and actively moving forward in their life? Personally, I find this type of person to be inspirational and charismatic. I strive to be this way. One of my best friends is moving ahead in her goal to buy a house, on her own. I am thrilled for her, and know that she will turn that place into a marvelous home, (the kind you can't wait to return to after a hard day), with or without a spouse.

Dragging our feet, waiting for someone to come along and propel us into fulfilling our dreams, is like expecting to win the lottery jackpot, but never buying a ticket. Being the type of woman who is on the move is one that many men will tend to openly chase. If you have pushed the pause button on living your life, hoping Mr. Right would come along and stir up the desire to live up to your potential, it is time to re-evaluate! What brings you joy? What are your gifts and talents? How could you use those gifts and talents to serve others? What are your dreams?

Jolt yourself out of apathy, and no longer play the waiting game! Stop letting your singleness be a convenient distraction from fulfilling your purpose and making a difference in this world. Maybe I am a romantic optimist, but I believe that love will come along when the timing is right, whether via the online dating route or by some other means.

The Guy's Perspective: Meet Mike and Jose

One very single Saturday night, I called my up friend Mike to ask if he wanted to go watch some bad singing, (Isn't all karaoke bad singing according to Simon Cowell?) drink a couple of Michelob Ultras, and swap dating war stories. I'd met Mike through Jenn, one of my closest friends in El Paso, and from the get-go we had a very comfortable friendship. Not complicated with romantic attraction (We are both Caucasian, and Mike likes Latin women, as I gravitate to Latin men), we'd always enjoyed laughs and great conversation.

After watching a couple of very drunk men sing "Push It" by Salt and Peppa, accompanied by questionable, and might I say, suggestive dance moves, Mike and I decided to leave our dive karaoke bar, and head to the nearest Village Inn restaurant for a late night coffee chat.

Somehow in the mix, the topic of this book arose, and he began gushing about how he absolutely must read it as soon as it was available, and that it sounded fascinating. He insisted that he needed a glance into what women were thinking, and how they viewed the men they were considering when checking out profiles on dating sites.

As we continued to laugh and joke about some of the unbelievable situations into which we had stumbled, we both had a sudden revelation!

What if Mike could insightfully comment on the way guys perceived what pictures women chose to represent themselves, how they wrote their profiles, and could candidly remark about both the good and bad impressions made by women? Spontaneously brainstorming there in the restaurant booth, the ideas were exploding like grenades! Within just a few minutes of light-hearted dialogue, I had learned so much!

While hashing these ideas over, I realized that while I could give advice based on circumstances that have happened to me, I would never possess the ability to "think like a man". So, after interviewing a willing and cooperative Mike (hey, men have to struggle through the online dating process too), I could only anticipate that his revelations would aid us as women in our plight to capture the attention of quality men. In light of this type of valuable information, we could analyze, and perhaps rethink at times, how to approach the online world, in hopes that we might truly put our "best feet forward", whether they are dainty and OPI painted, or badly in need of a pedicure.

This may be one of the most invaluable and practical sections of this book. I discovered that while I may have been spot-on with my suggestions, what women really need is to hear is the truth, about what they may be doing wrong, from those who are doing the judging and selecting, namely, the men! I decided to enlist the help of a couple of trustworthy men who could openly impart their advice and wisdom.

I chose two very different bachelors who would offer diversity in their opinions, due to their different life situations and duration of time they have been online daters.

Mike, who gave me the idea to include the male point of view, is a man in his mid 40's who was married for many years, and after several dismal set ups by friends, reluctantly threw his hat into the online arena. He is the type of man who would treat a woman with respect, and loves to be in committed relationships.

Once I had picked Mike's brain, I felt the urge to get the perspective of another seasoned online dater with whom I was friends. José is a very attractive guy in his mid 20s, who had become so frustrated with the singles scene in El Paso, that he mindfully tackled the online romance scene with a determination that he would find someone. I'd almost say that he treated it like a part-time job. He is incredibly intelligent, witty and sarcastic. We'd gone out a few times, but due to differing views on religion and politics, we'd ended up becoming friends instead trying to make a romantic connection work. There was no doubt that his insights would be blunt and to the point.

Please read on to uncover facts about what online men are looking for, that may otherwise slip our attention as women. We are constantly being told by our friends how great we are, how we are perfect, and how any guy who wouldn't want to be with us must be a fool. This may be true, or maybe we need to work on some things, but ultimately, we should try to have our profiles present to our cyber visitors how wonderful we truly are. Until they meet you, that is all they have to go by. I know that I was surprised at some of the guidance that Mike and José shared, but I am also grateful to pass this wisdom on to you.

MIKE'S Musings:

What do you think are the most common mistakes women make when creating their online profile?

What I really want to know is why every woman says in the first few lines of the profile that she wants to meet an honest, sincere man. Who is going to tell you that he is a liar, a deceiver, or a shallow guy with psychotic tendencies? Don't be naïve and dumb! We all want this type of person, but not everyone is going to be that. Also using the phrase, "I'm an independent woman who….." is just stereotypical and ordinary. Don't let your first two lines, which could either prompt the reader to continue reading or move on to the next profile, be a cheesy cliché. Stand out. Be clever.

The right kinds of profile pictures are critical when attempting to attract the right type of guy. The wrong photos can drive off men who could potentially be right for you.

For example, we have all seen the pictures where it is obvious the individual was with someone else, but they have cut the other person out. Men will immediately wonder who the hell was attached to you - A boyfriend? A husband? There have even been times when the man or woman in this type of photo is dressed really formally, which screams that you were out on a fancy date. Are we going to be rebound guys? Is there still emotional baggage tied to the cut-out picture chap? Do you keep the other half of the picture under your pillow, hoping that one day you might reconcile? It's tough to be in competition with the Invisible Man.

Also when you post a variety of party and club pics, and there always seems to be a drink in your hand, men looking for a serious relationship may pass you by. If these are the "shots" that represent you, they suggest that you are an excessive drinker and partier. The majority of men seeking lasting romance online are doing so because they are tired of the bar scene. So, if you are not always at the club, just post some different pictures in diverse settings, which show that you are well-rounded, or at the least, not simply a functioning alcoholic.

Truthfully, what really puzzles me are those pictures women post where they are standing in front of a mirror, sometimes at the bar, and it is obvious that they are in the bathroom. Gross!!! Please! No photos in the bathroom, ladies. I don't give a crap (pun intended), how much fun you are having with your crazy friends, this is a BIG turn off!

Try not to include pictures where you are with other guys, because other men will think they are potential competition. I know I will. Maybe I sound insecure, but remember, I don't know you yet. For all I know, that guy is either secretly in love with you, an ex you are not over, or a guy you had an obsessive crush on. In this situation I am between a rock and a hard place. If I ask you who the guy is, you will think I am over-possessive and jealous right off the bat. If I don't inquire, it will drive me to drink, and before you know it I will be taking pictures with my friends in the bathroom of a bar somewhere!

Listen up! Little tiny pictures are almost worse than no pictures at all! The whole point of the image is to reveal what you look like. When there is a tiny ant-like woman standing beside the Eiffel Tower, this is counterproductive. It is wonderful that you had the opportunity to visit such an exotic locale! However, I am not considering dating the Eiffel Tower, so it is not beneficial for me that you posted this photo. At times, I have passed over profiles simply because of this error.

Another point of frustration commences when you wear sunglasses in every photo you post. Are you in the witness protection program? Are you a fugitive, on the run from the law? They say that the eyes are the window to the soul. With those shades, we can't tell if you have bright fiery eyes or dead lifeless ones. To sum up, men want to see your face, and we want to see what body type you are.

Perhaps you think this is shallow, and maybe it is, but this is the truth. Maybe this isn't shallow at all, depending on your point of view. As a man, and a primarily visual creature, I can assure you that it is reality, even if men are not usually willing to voice these views out loud.

One more pet peeve that irritates us when viewing your profile is when you post pictures with friends, and then do not include a caption identifying who you are. At times, there will be entire groups, like class reunions, and although you provide us with the token red arrow, when we try to blow that part up for a closer look, you look like a blurry ghost. Looking at a profile should not feel like investigative reporting, so please humor us and provide pictures that give us a realistic idea of what you look like!

Written Copy in Profile

What you write in your profile greatly influences that potential date, who will be contemplating whether he wants to attempt to contact you based on what you disclose about yourself.

Disclaimer: Please understand that I do not discriminate against those whose first language may not be English. With that being said, it is important to note that written text in your profile should not be written in broken English. Ex: I cook good. This could make a man uneasy, and he might feel a little like he's shopping for a Russian mail-order bride.

Keep in mind that you need to be able to fluently communicate with your potential soul-mate if you truly plan to get to know him, therefore a basic mastery of English (or another language you both know well) should be a prerequisite.

One of the greatest personal pet peeves I have about what a woman has written in her profile is when she constantly uses "text speak": OMG, ROTFL, cuz, u, etc…. Really? You are a 40 year old woman, and you can't write the word "you" instead of using the letter? Texting didn't even exist when you were in your 20's! This overused written slang is not impressive.

While I'm at it, let me also state that not being able to spell, use punctuation, or show a basic functional usage of the English language, will not showcase you as the intelligent woman I'm sure you are. Even people who are spelling or grammar "challenged" deserve love too! Ask a trustworthy friend to help edit your profile if you know that written English is NOT your strength. Friends, don't let friends, post error ridden profiles!

When asked how much information to provide when creating a profile, I would say that it is best to share some unique facts about yourself without giving away too many details, so there is some mystery left. What will you have to talk about over dinner if you have already revealed everything about yourself on your profile? It can be a little overwhelming when people have read the equivalent to your un-abridged autobiography on your page. Trying to remember all of those details in an effort to ask insightful questions about them on a first date, is a lot of pressure! You need to make those who are interested in getting to know you work for it, and provide them with only enough detail in your profile to spark some curiosity.

What would you say are the top three parts of a profile that most men would look at, that weigh in on whether they contact a woman or not?

I would say that one of the first details that I inspect is a woman's income/job situation. This is not because I am looking at you to become my sugar mamma. What this information does is provide me with an idea about the goals, motivation, and drive you may or may not possess. Whether you have various college degrees is not my main concern, but I need to know that you are responsible and dependable enough to hold down a respectable job! If I am held to this standard, then you should be too! If you can't feed your 3 babies, what makes you think I will be willing or able to?

Some women seem to be online looking for men to take care of them. Most guys want to feel they are part of a team, a partnership, and that includes the area of finances.

I'm not speaking on behalf of all mankind here, but politics would definitely be one of the top three issues on which my date and I would need to click. This is due to the fact that I am super-liberal, and if a woman holds beliefs that are in complete opposition to mine, this would be a mountain we could not conquer.

At the risk of being hated by many women in America, I would have to say that body type is another factor for me as I weigh in on (pun intended) whether a woman would be right for me. I have a weight limit rule - I will never date a woman who weighs as much as I do. When you see these women you know they automatically expect to be taken to restaurants; you know they didn't get that fat going on hiking dates.

All kidding aside, I really am concerned about if a woman is going to be active and enjoy the fast-paced lifestyle that I do. Let's be honest, women, we know that you care about the fitness of your potential date as well. Those fireman calendars are not buying themselves. As I mentioned earlier, guys are visual creatures, and we do make judgments based on appearance. If a man says he doesn't, then he is not one of those "honest and sincere men" so many of you say you are seeking in your descriptions.

Although Karen only asked me for the top three factors that we men consider while perusing your profile, I would like to go ahead and add one more for your consideration. We almost all check to see if you have children. It is not a deal breaker for many of us if you do have kids, but there is a "load limit". If you mention that you have never been married and you have 3 kids, this does raise a BIG RED FLAG. Whether it is fair or not, we wonder why you did not end up with the baby daddy or baby daddies. As far as naming 3 children as my personal limit… even if my kids aren't with me, my truck only holds 5 and I am not buying a suburban to haul you and your pack around town. If you were not married, then it is likely no child support is coming in. We wonder if you are a broke woman looking for a sugar daddy… and how many dads are even in the picture anyway? Are any of those guys crazy, incarcerated, or have outstanding restraining orders? These are common and legitimate questions running through our minds as we read about your "kid situation".

What suggestions could you make to women who are genuinely looking for love rather than hookups, as to how they should represent themselves online?

If in your photo you are showing so much cleavage that it looks like a bicycle rack where you could park your bike, it is too much. Why are you putting everything out there? You are not even making him work for it! I have also been confused when I see obese women, who have thighs looking like hams hanging in a butcher shop, proudly showing them off in their short skirts.

Usually there is a section that shows how often you drink alcohol. If you put that you drink frequently or daily that is crazy, or at least it makes you look crazy. This is something you do not want to advertise. All that I have picked up from you sharing that you are living your life under the fog of a continual buzz, is that you need Dr. Drew rather than me.

Now you may be asking, after hearing all this negative feedback, how should you go about presenting yourself as a viable love interest? First, try to show your sense of humor in a friendly, informal way. Sound approachable. You could start by just writing a guy a short note, and he would most likely respond positively. If you are not interested in someone who has winked or emailed you, just move on. There is no reason to email him and tell them why. In fact, it might just save the guy a bruised ego if you say nothing. He might not even remember contacting you, so there is no need to hurt his feelings!

What do you think is appropriate timing when it comes to communicating, and then actually meeting in person? Can you provide a realistic timeline?

I really like the instant message feature, due to my need for instant gratification. This venue also helps to get a sense of who this person is as she responds to my questions. If all goes well, it makes sense to exchange a few emails. By about the third email, I will typically offer up my phone number if the woman wants it. Just the fact that I have spent this much time and energy staying in contact with anyone in particular, means that on some level, I am unquestionably interested.

Maybe it's because I am from the old school, but I would prefer to jump straight to calls, rather than waste time texting. This type of communication feels somewhat impersonal, and if your humor is not understood, you can come off as a jerk. Once this bridge from electronic to personal communication has been crossed, I would say it is best to not have too many phone calls before you decide to go out. Set up the time and then see what happens on the date! Of course, if someone is seeking love out of town, multiple phone calls cannot be avoided.

When meeting in person for the first time, what do you think most men would consider a good first date? Where would you suggest meeting?

I would be skeptical of any man who tries to persuade you to meet anywhere but a public place. Even if you have communicated at length, you still have not actually met, and he is still a stranger.

A restaurant is a fitting place to talk, or even grab a quick cup of coffee. Movies are terrible places for a first date because there is little interaction. It is better not to plan something too elaborate, but rather keep it simple to avoid pressure.

What are your pet peeves about women who are on online dating sites?

Women's standards are so high. It is not really fair to complain about this because, as men, we have the same high standards. What do we do about this standoff? No one wants to settle or lower their standards. What it comes down to is what types of idiosyncrasies and differences are you willing to tolerate?

A pet peeve of mine is that sometimes the women who pop up in your search results don't adhere to your stated criteria….maybe the various online dating sites are trying to get you to broaden your horizons, but it feels like they are forcing you to give up on finding the type of person with whom you feel you truly belong.

Also, when no picture is posted on a woman's profile, it is a source of frustration for me. I assume she is possibly a 300 pound hunch-back with missing teeth. Otherwise, I figure she is probably married or otherwise attached, and doesn't want her significant other to know she is still wading in the forbidden waters of dating.

Another pet peeve I have concerning the women I meet online is when I hear from someone a few times, and then she just disappears. What happened? It is like, "Hey! I'll call you," and then you never hear from her again. Seriously, it's just not ok to play with someone's heart. It ends up feeling like just one more rejection - especially if she seemed legitimately interested at first. It's unfair not to let the person you've been in regular contact with know what went wrong. Maybe a subscription expired? Maybe there was a family crisis? Or maybe, just maybe, the interest perceived just wasn't there. It's only common courtesy to let a person know what happened.

Pet peeves about the dating websites themselves

Why is it these online dating sites do not post whether or not the profile is current, or if the people using them have up-to-date subscriptions? It is inconsiderate to those seriously seeking love.

Also, I've noticed that once you cancel your subscription, suddenly, they send you the names of all these women who are "interested" in you. Part of me believes they are decoys sent to hook you back in. How do I know this is likely? Once you decide to cave and add another month to your membership, these women mysteriously disappear! You might think I am being paranoid, but this seems deceptive, and maybe even deliberate.

If a woman were to see your profile and be really interested in getting to know you, what would you consider to be too aggressive an approach?

I would be wary if she immediately requested my phone number or wanted to meet me right away. If she wrote me super-long emails right off the bat, that would also make me uncomfortable. Any contact from you is supposed to be more like the trailer to a movie or the back page of a book cover - meant to tease and arouse curiosity. I should feel a need and drive to discover more. Too much information too quickly comes off as a little desperate.

Do you think most men are in contact with more than one woman at a time?

Let me ask you this - Ladies, am I the only guy you have been viewing? I didn't think so. On Match.com we each get sent 5 shots, I mean potential bachelorettes, every day with the Daily Interest feature. No double standard. It's like buying a car at a used car lot. Are you really only considering one car?

A red one? An SUV or a sports car? Are you kind of excited that there are many people who are potentially available? During this time in your life you get to be a player......well, sort of. Only James Bond gets to walk into the club, and exit with a dozen hot girls hanging on his arm.

What are the ways that you utilize a dating site? What functions do you use the most? Search? Quick Match? Who's on?

I like the Daily Interest, Quick Match, and Viewing Profile functions on the various sites. They aid in guiding me through potential matches. I'm not willing to pay any extra fees for them to highlight my profile so it stands out, or to see immediately when a woman reads my carefully crafted email. It is 9:45 am when she read my message, and it is now 10:45, but she hasn't responded yet? That is a lot to keep track of! This seems over the top, and who really has that much time on their hands, anyway?

Do you believe that love can truly be found online, or are you a skeptic?

I'm skeptical - It hasn't happened for me yet, and I've tried for almost two years. I'm still not comfortable telling people about it, because I don't want to seem desperate. It was actually my ex-mother-in-law who sparked my interest in investigating online options for dating.

To me, it still feels like a stigma is attached to this process. Once, someone actually asked me if I was looking for a mail-order-bride. Sometimes I think people secretly wonder why I can't just meet someone naturally, without the help of a computer. Even though I have an excellent education, well paying job, and am reasonably attractive, it makes me feel inadequate that 300 people look at my profile and don't respond.

José's Two Cents Worth: The Young Buck's Quest for Love.

What do you think are the most common mistakes women make when creating their online profiles?

I suppose it depends on how you define "mistake," but I tend to instantly ignore or skip over profiles that contain an inordinate amount of spelling and/or grammatical errors. I think people tend to forget that a dating profile is a way for them to represent themselves to the world, and when you can't even bother to proofread your profile, you are sending the message that you are inattentive, or worse, unintelligent.

Similarly, if you're an adult and still using abbreviations like "2" for "to" or "4" for "for," you might consider forgetting online dating and instead enroll in an English class at the local community college. I realize I may fall into a minority group by feeling this way, but these kinds of things matter.

Another red flag for me is when a person mentions a previous relationship in their profile. If you are still feeling bitterness or resentment about the way your previous relationship ended, especially to the point where you are mentioning it in your profile, you should re-evaluate whether or not you're ready to start dating again. If I know why you broke up with your ex and I've never even met you, chances are you are exuding way too much crazy for me to even consider messaging you.

Lastly, photos, or lack thereof, can make or break a profile. Ostensibly, you're on a dating site to meet people, so not having a photo up is a bit like showing up to a single's party in a traditional burqa. You want to have at least one good photo of your face, and preferably one that shows you in your entirety. Some of you might think, "I don't want guys to judge me just on my looks," but this is just one of those things you want to get out of the way as soon as possible. Striking up a conversation with someone and then finding out that you're not really that attracted to them, is one of those painful things that ruins online dating.

Oh, and please, no pictures of your cat. If you're going to put up pictures of your cat, you may as well just go get a jump on your porcelain doll collection instead of messing around with online dating.

What would you consider to be the top three things that most men will look at first on a woman's profile page?

This is incredibly subjective and personal, but my top 3 are:

Her sense of humor. A well-written, witty profile is incredibly attractive to intelligent men. Profiles that consist of platitudes such as "I like to have fun", tend to make me want to close my browser and toss my computer out the window.

Her looks. I wish I could say something uplifting here that would make my gender seem less superficial, but the sad truth is that even those of us looking for an intelligent, long-term partner are going to care about looks. Most of us don't expect a beauty queen, so this generally boils down to whether or not she takes care of herself. Does she like to exercise? Does she seem to have good hygiene? These things say a lot about a person.

I can't think of third criteria.

What suggestions can you make to women who are genuinely looking for love rather than hookups, as to how they should represent themselves online?

This seems pretty obvious and has some parallels with real life. If your profile contains mostly pictures of you in skimpy clothing, or God forbid, the gratuitous boob shot, don't be surprised when all you get are monosyllabic messages inviting you to film a porno.

What do you think is appropriate timing when it comes to communicating, and then actually meeting in person? Can you provide a realistic timeline?

My friends and I like to call this the "serial killer factor." Some women behave in a sketchy manner online, and those are the ones I am most hesitant to contact immediately.

Author's Note: As José has successfully fallen in love, with someone he met online; he never got back to me with the answers to the last few questions of the interview. He and his significant other have now been together for over six months. Apparently, there are happy endings for us online dating hopefuls, so be encouraged ladies and gentlemen!

The Happy Ending to My Online Dating Saga?

I HAD COME CLOSE TO abandoning the idea of meeting someone with whom I could spend the rest of my life online. This journey had been long and grueling. Sure, I had heard of others who had successfully managed to meet the loves of their lives, and had gone on to begin their once elusive "happily ever afters". Yet with the various experiences I have shared with you and the many I have probably even mentally BLOCKED from memory, my patience for dating on the World Wide Web was rapidly waning. I was starting to believe that lasting connections online were more urban myth than reality. The mail in my inboxes was piling up, the winks were a mountain high, and it appeared that I had finally had enough. I had begun to wave the white flag of surrender, even though I had not wanted to admit it to myself.

Even those men who'd appeared to have some potential, and lived locally, did not cause my heart to beat faster with any kind of anticipation. Half-heartedly, I would look at the winks and mail that I received, and usually not even acknowledge to the senders that I had ever laid eyes on them. In the few cases in which I even responded by jotting a few lines back to someone, I always seemed to drop the ball and not follow through afterward. Some of the more persistent gentleman would write to me a few more times, patiently asking if I had been too busy to respond. I had to admire their tenacity, but more often than not, I would avoid revealing much of myself, or showing much interest in them.

My friend José had chastised me once when he'd found out I was not replying to each online suitor, but at the risk of sounding obnoxious, I'd patiently explained to him that it would have been like juggling a part time job. Due to my teacher's life of grading papers and lesson planning, often even at night and during weekends, free time just seemed too precious to waste on getting all dolled up to go and meet strangers anymore. Curling up with a good mystery novel, sipping some hot coffee, even going to the gym, seemed more appealing than any more online blind dates!

I still remember the Sunday night when I encountered Fernando. It was in the middle of May, and there were only a few weeks left of the hectic school year. Summer was quickly approaching, and I could finally see the light at the end of the tunnel. Perhaps this relief was what had prodded me to go back to the original Christian dating website suggested to me by my mother, on our Mexican vacation more than a decade before! Procrastinating seemed to be a better option than working on lesson plans, so I went onto one site that I had not visited for at least a month or two. Finding the men with profiles on that site to be either very far away, too young, or in other ways incompatible with me, had discouraged me from focusing much attention on seriously considering any of them.

As mentioned in my Online Tips section of this book, it is wise to use the "Who's Online" feature on a website, because that way you are likely to get a wink, email, or even occasionally an instant message via the chat feature. That evening, I'd started to browse, and had seen a very unusual picture - an artistic one of an attractive Latino man. Talk to any of my friends or family members and they will tell you that I have always thought Latin men were the most eye-catching of the male species. Even though he had not filled out his profile short answers, I could see that he was new to the website, so I assumed that he'd probably put off answering all those daunting and intrusive questions. He was 38 (closer in age than many of the men I dated), and seemed alarmingly ....normal! I decided to send him a wink. That way, if he read my profile and was at all interested, he could shoot a wink back at me, or write me a note.

Looking back, if that was all he had done, it may never have gone any further. I had stopped visiting this site regularly, and his trial with this venue, as I'd found out later, would have expired within days. By the time I may have received his response and written back, he would most likely not have been able to even read my note. Everything may have come to a screeching halt. We could have been like two ships passing each other on a foggy night, never encountering one another.

At this point, I personally believed that God intervened in the story. For those of you who do not share my beliefs, I understand your doubt, but remember that one of the largest dating obstacles for me was finding someone with who I could share my beliefs and faith. Love had become so evasive, as slippery as a wet bar of soap, for so long. Even though I believed that God had someone for me, doubt had crept in like an unwanted mosquito, buzzing in my ear.

Just minutes before I was about to log off, I received an instant message. Opening it up, I realized it was from the attractive man at whom I had winked. We started to chat, and it was evident that conversation was easy and required little effort. Right away, we started to joke around with each other, and even though I could tell that English was his second language, we were still able to communicate well, and I had the chance to practice my rusty Spanish! Mr. Attractive had a name, and it was Fernando. He was living just outside of San Francisco - one of the most beautiful places in the U.S. As we continued to interact, I found out that he was divorced with one child, a boy who was 7 years old.

He impressed me with how well-rounded and exotic he was, and how engrossed he was in asking me questions. An hour had passed before we even knew it, and his computer battery was on its last legs. Knowing I had some materials that I had to prepare for class the next day, we had come to <u>that</u> moment. That moment of setting up *whether* we would ever communicate again. For those of you out there in the online dating world, I believe you know exactly "the instant" I am talking about. After a time of chatting, you feel a spark, but don't want to come across as being too aggressive or desperate when addressing the possibility of future communication.

When Fernando mentioned he would enjoy getting to know me further, I decided to go for broke and gave him my phone number so he could text me. I explained to him that at this time of the school year I usually did not have time to be online, so it would be unlikely that we would randomly run into each other by chance. Being coy and elusive was simply not going to be effective in this situation, so I decided to put the ball in his court, and if he felt that I was being too forward, so be it. What did I have to lose? Please note, I am aware that in this situation I did not take my own advice about not giving out my phone number so soon, but what can I say? Sometimes I like to go with my gut and break the rules!

The next night I received a text from Fernando and from that point on, we started texting throughout the day (not during school hours, except at lunch). As the days went on, we would text and occasionally talk on the phone. He was charming, considerate, funny, and entertaining to speak to. Not long into the phone calls, we had decided that we definitely would enjoy meeting each other in person. Normally this suggestion so soon into an online connection would have made me feel skittish, even uncomfortable. In this case, however, I was hopeful and really eager to meet this man in person.

Apparently, I was the first person Fernando had wanted to seriously pursue since his divorce the year before.

I had already arranged to fly into Seattle, Washington instead of Vancouver, British Columbia, a week and a half after school let out. We decided that we could meet in Seattle; I would just stay a few extra days there to hang out with Fernando, before taking the 3 hour airport shuttle back home. This would give us some time to see if the connection that was present on the phone would also be there in person.

Would we have that necessary chemistry? Pictures are hard to decipher. Fernando looked completely different in all three photos he had posted on his profile. Before you judge me for being superficial, please know that a man's heart and character are a large part of what makes him attractive to me. However, my mother had passed a piece of advice on to me in high school, when I was not sure of whether to give one particular love-struck classmate a chance. Her exact words were, "It is great if you like a young man's personality, but you don't have to kiss his personality goodnight."

Before I knew it, Fernando had purchased his airline ticket, and it was official! Due to my very busy schedule, and extended hours at school, there were nights where I had already anticipated that it would be hard to speak to him on the phone much before the trip. There was not an instance when he demanded to talk to me, or tried to convince me that I could take a break and blow off the work I had to do. Although this budding friendship made me happy, part of me was potentially guarding my heart in case, for some reason, it didn't work out….again.

What I was not aware of during this time, was that Fernando was feeling a little frustrated with the lack of phone communication. This was understandable, as he had been in a ten year marriage which had only ended the previous year, and this was his first serious attempt to enter the realm of the online dating scene.

He had not yet experienced the many disappointments with potential loves that I had. He had not had his feelings hurt, when suddenly, the person with whom he was communicating did not respond to his emails, because she was focused more on some other man she had met online. He had not invested the time in getting to know someone, only to find when finally he was able to meet her, the chemistry was inexplicably absent. He had not been lied to and deceived by an online suitor, and made to feel like a fool.

Looking back, knowing Fernando the way I do now, I feel guilty that I was not more enthusiastic and self-sacrificing. Within two weeks, he had sent an absolutely exquisite bouquet of pink roses to my school. There was no special occasion. He did this for no reason but to express how much he was enjoying getting to know me. My hormonal seventh grade students went wild, and were full of questions and curiosity about my new beau.

A few nights later, Fernando confronted me with a question that shocked me to the core. We had been texting that day, but had not spoken on the phone, and right before I was going to turn out my light and go to sleep, I got the text with the loaded question. "Karen, do you think that you have space in your life for a man?" In disbelief, I wondered if he was going the same route as some of the other men in whom I had been interested, and was about to pull a disappearing act, while conveniently blaming the mess on me!

My first reaction was shock, which rapidly developed into hurt and anger. My immediate response to him was "You sent me flowers this week, and now you don't think that things are working?"

His texts conveyed a calm tone, if that was possible. He went on to explain that he knew that I was busy, did not want to be demanding and unreasonable, but wanted to be sure that my life was one into which a man could fit. Bringing up that I lived alone and had not been married before, he wondered if I was perhaps happy with the routine of my life, and set in my ways. Looking back now, I remember that I adamantly disagreed, and told him I was going to make time to talk with him more often.

Throughout the week however, the question nagged and taunted me, as I considered whether at this stage in my life Fernando had a valid point. Was I more in love with the idea of love, or was I willing to make concessions and an active effort to develop this relationship into something with more substance? After discussing this with a few of my best friends who know me well, I was able to come to the conclusion that for the RIGHT man, I would be a great partner: an encourager, a fun person to hang out with, and a fiercely loyal and faithful spouse. Many women out there who have been single and lived on their own for any length of time, can relate to the fact that when you have no other personal responsibilities besides looking after yourself, it takes time to adjust to the thought of serving someone else, considering their needs as well as your own, and making compromises. Maybe I would be able to even hand over the remote control every once in a while for the right man!

I decided to dive in and make sure that I did not sacrifice what could have been a very healthy potential relationship for a lack of effort on my part. The more I called him, the more I enjoyed our flirty and fun conversations. Soon, I absolutely could not wait for the time when I would get a chance to finally meet him.

The school year ended, and the day had come when I would arrive in Seattle. When I hesitantly told my dad that I was going to meet Fernando on my way home, he seemed genuinely happy for me, even saying that maybe the reason I had not secured the teaching job I had previously pursued in San Antonio, was because I was possibly going to end up meeting someone!

Meanwhile, Fernando had spoken with his mom in Columbia, and she had sounded enthusiastic about the news that he was meeting me. Already, we seemed to have preliminary parental approval of our endeavor. My mom had even failed to mention, even once, that Fernando could've been a potential serial killer or a sleazy con artist!

About two weeks before we met, we had become Facebook friends, which presented Fernando with the opportunity to view approximately a thousand pictures of me: the good, the bad, and the sweaty (any picture from my summer missions trip to Hong Kong was one where I was perspiring!). Part of me worried that he would find that he would not be attracted to me after all, and I remember once I added him to my friends, I apprehensively waited for a text from him. Finally, I received one, and the first words I read were, "You are so pretty Karen, even more beautiful than I thought." A confident girl still needs to feel that her prospective love interest thinks she is attractive, and I recall exhaling a sigh of relief. When I opened up his pictures, I realized that there really were not many more than what I had already seen on his dating profile. Not to mention that he was not smiling in any of them! Although this concerned me slightly, I felt that I enjoyed his personality enough, that if there happened to be no physical chemistry, I would actually want to be friends with him anyway.

The night before the trip almost felt like Christmas Eve, and I was surprised that I did not feel as nervous or anxious as I imagined I would. After a month of communicating, I was about to embark on a first date with a gentleman I had grown to know, and grown to care for, via phone and text. This was not an hour coffee date at Starbucks, but a two and a half day long rendezvous! Operating on about four hours of sleep, I arrived in Seattle wondering how I would locate Fernando. After darting into the restroom to quickly retouch my makeup and brush my hair, the moment had come to head down to baggage claim to collect my suitcases and my date!

Since all of his pictures made him look somewhat different, I was relying on the fact that he had seen enough pictures of me that I would be undeniably recognizable. Also, it has been my experience that there are not an over abundance of 6"4' Latin men out there, so this would potentially tip me off to his identity. I watched as people rushed around, looked for loved ones, tried to figure out on which carousel their luggage would hopefully make an appearance, and generally scurried from gate to gate.

As I made my way down the escalator which seemed to be moving in extreme slow motion, I tried inconspicuously to glance at any tall male who would fit Fernando's description.

Suddenly, I spotted him on the other side of baggage claim. Recognition had already registered on his face, and finally I was able to see a smile beaming at me. Later I would find out that he had spotted me first, had known who I was immediately, and had felt very excited that we were finally going to hang out in person! As this man came closer and closer, my heart almost pounded out of my chest. He rushed over to me, gave me a bear hug, and brushed a tender kiss on my cheek. Even though there must have been a multitude of travelers around, at that moment, it felt as if we were the only two people in the entire airport! Not only was Fernando attractive, but he was truly one of the best looking men I had ever seen up close.

It was overwhelming how drawn to him I was. He was alarmingly tall, had a muscular and lanky frame - my favorite, and the most soft, beautiful brown eyes I had ever seen. I know I am gushing, and I apologize, but I am not even going to mention his chiseled and manly face or his salt and pepper clean cut hair. We walked over to the baggage carousel, chatting and laughing with each other. I found myself distracted by his good looks, and had to pull myself together. "Calm down!" I silently reprimanded in my head, "Just enjoy Fernando's company, and be yourself.

It appeared to me that Fernando was genuinely thrilled to meet me, and that put me at ease. Mercifully, my bags were a few of the first to appear, and before I could even decide how to maneuver them, he had already brought me a cart, hardly allowing me to carry anything. For a woman who is accustomed to traveling alone, and hauling her mountains of heavy luggage around herself, this was a treat that I could definitely see myself getting used to.

I vaguely remember walking to the rental car, and, at this point, I could not relay what we talked about. Part of me knew I needed to listen in case Fernando was telling me something that I would be expected to remember later, but I felt almost hypnotized. Staring at him, I found myself just taking in this person I had spent so much time communicating with via phone and text. "Give the impression of being appropriately interested Rissling, not stalker level interested!" I silently chided myself. In the car, we chatted and bonded until we realized that our rental car's GPS system was not working. Just perfect for two strangers unfamiliar with Seattle!

As we sped down the road, it seemed hard for either of us to focus on reaching our destination. We were still taking in the fact that we were finally physically together! I guess it goes without saying, that without a map or a functional GPS we were immediately lost while trying to find our hotel. At gas station number one, I asked directions, but I was so nervous in the presence of the tall, gorgeous man next to me, that I failed to take down the correct information.

Even on a good day I am directionally impaired, but add to the equation that I was trying not to appear to be a complete navigational moron, and my chicken scratch writing ended up being undecipherable. As Fernando was driving, I realized that I had no idea which way we should go, and I was starting to tense up. As if able to read my mind, he gently put his large, soft hand over mine for a moment, squeezed it and murmured, "It's ok Karen, don't worry." At the touch of his hand, I felt an almost physical shock of attraction for him, as well as immediate relief.

This was when I was able to inhale deeply, release the pressure of impressing him, and know that we'd simply get directions at the next gas station. The surprise though, was that I was about to experience my first kiss with Fernando in that gas station! While grabbing two diet sodas from the back of the store, he'd asked me a question and I'd looked up at him, listening intently. Before I knew it, in front of several strangers picking up their convenience store coffee and paying for their gas, Fernando bent down, and gently kissed me on the lips. How unexpected, I thought. This gesture reassured me that this handsome man was, in fact, interested and attracted to me, and that was exactly what I had needed to feel so I could relax.

To this day, Fernando teases me that I was the initiator of that kiss, but that would have been an impossible feat for two reasons. First of all, he towers over me at 6"4', so there was no way I could even reach up that high to plant a big juicy one on his lips. A second point to consider is that I was still feeling a bit shy and unsure about what he was feeling, so I would <u>never</u> in a million years have risked a possible rejection with such a brazen move! My momma always said to let the men make the moves and pursue you, and those are words by which I have always lived! As it turned out, the chemistry between us was electric. You could light a fire with the spark!

The next few days were a whirlwind of strolling the streets of Seattle, chatting and sightseeing. The whole experience almost felt like a dream from which I never wanted to wake up. At the end of our time together, we decided to define our relationship as exclusively "dating" to see where it would lead. I called him the second night after I got home, and by this time he had already stated in a text that he loved me. This declaration might have seemed premature, however, when we'd considered the fact that love is more of a decision than just a fleeting emotion, it just seemed like the natural next step to take.

Every night we would talk for at least 2 to 3 hours, and I was eternally (and financially) grateful that my Canadian parents had a free unlimited phone plan to the U.S.

The next meeting was in mid-July, when I flew to San Francisco to spend time seeing where my new boyfriend lived, and have a glimpse into his everyday life. The area was beautiful with spectacular beaches, trees, rolling hills, and views that stole my breath away. There is something about seeing a man on his turf that creates a more accurate picture of what your life could look like with him. I was beginning to sense that if things were to progress the way they had been, that I could actually envision a future together.

A highlight for me was enjoying a nice lunch, and walking along the shoreline in Half Moon Bay, a quaint "beachy" town that had more than enough charm to rival any Nicholas Sparks novel setting! On our way home Fernando had stopped at a Baskin Robbins for some ice-cream. When we returned to the vehicle, we discovered that he had locked the keys inside. We could see them dangling in the ignition, impossible to reach. Just as he was about to call his boss, since he had borrowed the work van, I casually mentioned that we should check and see if there was a magnetic key box hidden somewhere underneath, close to the wheels. Miraculously we found one, and were able to get in and carry on with our day.

Fernando had not freaked out when he had discovered his unlucky error. He had not had a temper tantrum nor lost his cool. He was so even-tempered and easy to be around, that we always enjoyed our time with one another. When we were together we seemed able to avoid those relationship pot-holes that can cause wear and tear on a couple: there was no drama, having to analyze puzzling behaviors, arguing, or hurt feelings. Not having to question myself, not having to over-analyze how I was feeling, and knowing that this man was committed to me despite experiencing my imperfections, was a freeing sensation that I had not known for years!

Meeting Fernando's friends, Miguel and Rosa, for dinner near the end of my 4 day stay, initially caused a bit of anxiety. What if they didn't like me or thought that I was not right for him? I knew that Spanish would be the dominant language spoken that evening, and I wondered if I would be able to understand all that was being said and be able to respond appropriately.

It turned out to be a wonderful evening, and I immediately felt accepted. Their smiles and words warmed me like a cozy pair of mittens on a cold day. Having a chance to meet people who cared about him, helped me feel that I knew Fernando more intimately.

At one point in the evening Miguel had made a comment that caught my attention. It almost seemed to suggest that he thought that Fernando needed to get his life in order before becoming serious about a woman. He was referring to how work had been sporadic for Fernando, which had become a nagging concern of mine. Understanding that Miguel subscribed to a more traditional school of thought that the man should be the main provider, I chose not to overanalyze the remark at the time.

Sure, during my trip to San Francisco we went on excursions throughout the area, and I was able to take in the sights of the area, but ultimately it was not important what we did or where we went, as long as we were able to spend time together.

As we said our goodbyes at the airport this time, even though I knew I was going to miss Fernando, the fact that we had already discussed our upcoming encounter in El Paso, helped me to accept the separation.

My friend, Jenny, and I had planned a trip to Puerto Vallarta, and when it arrived, I wondered how Fernando would react to not having the 2 hour nightly calls or as much daily contact. As it turned out, he was incredibly thoughtful, without being overtly needy. I had given him my hotel information so he would know where I was staying and would be able to get in touch with me, if needed. Arriving at our beautiful (and upgraded) suite, I discovered that he had already left me a message, simply telling me to have a good time and that he missed me. The following day was my 40th birthday, and I returned to my room after a fun day at the beach to discover that

Fernando had sent me a beautiful, life-sized bouquet of exotic flowers. Since he had already presented me with a fantastic camera as a birthday present when I was visiting in California, I'd had no idea that he would make the extra effort to be so considerate and thoughtful. Forty is a birthday that most women struggle with, including me. Fernando made me feel beautiful, loved, and content on a day that had the potential to be very depressing!

It was apparent that I must be in love, as I did not notice men around me at all on this trip. Some of my vacation flirtations are legendary, as to which my friends will attest. Many shirtless and drool-worthy men crossed my path, and it was Jenny who would point them out, since I didn't seem to notice. Those who would attempt to talk to me, often asking how I had learned Spanish as their opening pick up line, would be forced to hear how my dreamy Columbian boyfriend would speak to me in this sonorous language.

On one particular morning, after returning from this relaxing and decadent trip, I'd had a chance to speak to my dad alone. I had mentioned the flowers to him, and he had asked, "So are you serious about Fernando?" I'd told him that I was, and asked if there was any way that he and Mom might be able to meet him in San Francisco over the Christmas break. My dad thought it sounded like a great idea, and told me that as the time drew nearer for me to return to the United States, he would bring it up to my mom, so we could all agree on a plan.

As we were discussing this, I was surprised to find that throughout the year while I had been frantically plotting my escape route from El Paso to San Antonio; my dad had not felt right about the move. In fact, he even mentioned that after hearing of my job hunting plans, he had been praying that if it was God's will, that I would not be put in a position to have to start over in a new city, not knowing anyone. Enter Fernando stage left. Looking back now, I feel that the Lord knew that I needed to be ready to leave El Paso, and this was my practice run of trying to apply to districts and paring down my belongings. For me, change is about as easy as passing up the perfect pair of shoes. Not a fan.

During this unplanned heart to heart with my dad, I was happy to see that not only did he seem supportive of this relationship, but my mom also seemed "optimistic" about it. Anyone who knows my mom is well aware that any man dating me with serious intentions would have to meet the challenge of winning over the family matriarch.

My dad is a piece of cake when it comes to accepting a potential suitor. Basically, all you need to win his affection is some type of food item, and if it is something sweet, like a Snickers bar…..you're in! I once had a boyfriend who my mom knew was dead wrong for me the entire time we were together. (But did I listen?) However, because this boyfriend worked at a pizza joint and would bring my dad the leftovers, they were as thick as thieves! I actually think he mourned that breakup more than I did!

With some trepidation during this chat with Dad, I finally ventured to ask if Mom had approached him with concerns and fears regarding my relationship with Fernando. I was almost flinching as I awaited his reply. His response was that Mom was ok with it, and even appeared "positive". This was astounding news! Usually when my mom doesn't want to address a situation directly, she will either talk to my dad when I am not around, or less subtly, loudly and purposefully express her doubts to him while I am somewhere I can eavesdrop!

When the time came for me to return to my educator's life in El Paso, I was faced with several unexpected political hassles and stressors thanks to a new school district superintendent. Bigger class sizes was the most daunting obstacle to be faced, as my largest class had students literally overflowing from the room. Add to the mix that I had students with learning challenges and language issues, and I felt more like a police officer than a teacher. It was getting to me. Even thoughts of other potential career options started running through my mind, which was unusual and discouraging. I loved teaching, but the circumstances I found myself in began to feel unbearable.

During the few times I lost it and lamented to Fernando about what was happening at work, he was such a rock for me. Supportive. Caring. Helpful. I was so grateful to have a person who was undeniably on my side, but would still challenge me to be rational and trust God. I just kept thinking that he was the perfect boyfriend for me. The cynical side of me which might have questioned this more, seemed to be silenced whenever it came to Fernando. I could not pinpoint anything that made me doubt that the relationship could be anything less than what we had envisioned - a fantastic courtship before marriage.

Within days of my arrival in El Paso, Fernando flew in to spend some time with me, and we had the chance to just exist together in the same place. All couples battling the dreaded long distance predicament understand what a luxury time together is. I was truly feeling spoiled during this time. I never felt that I wanted Fernando to leave or even needed a break from him. Love continued to grow in my heart for this Columbian Prince Charming.

After he returned home, the long stretch between August and the end of September (when we had planned our next meeting) was rough, and we missed each other terribly. I was so eager to see him again that I had purchased my ticket to go visit him almost immediately after Fernando had returned to the Sunshine State.

The relationship seemed to be moving along smoothly, even though it could argued at an accelerated pace, because of the distance. We did what many other "locationally challenged" couples do: had set phone dates, texted throughout the day, and made the best of a less than desirable circumstance.

Every night we would talk on the phone. One night Fernando became very jealous when I tried to call him earlier than usual due to the fact that I had arranged to spend the night at my friend Colleen's house. He'd assumed I was "getting the call out of the way," so I could go out on a double date with Colleen and a guy that she had met for coffee. This assumption was so completely out of the realm of logic that I was at a loss for how to reason with him. This was a side of Fernando that I never knew even existed! He overreacted dramatically, even telling me that he just couldn't take it anymore, and couldn't be in a long distance relationship. What was most unbelievable was how his voice sounded ice-cold and emotionless. Was I still speaking to Fernando, my potential husband? I remember crying so hard on the phone that I could barely speak, or breathe for that matter. Somewhere in my memory, which is fuzzy now, I remember him telling me to calm down. Calm down?! The man I loved was telling me that this relationship was obviously not nearly as important to him as it was to me. This demonstrated a lack of desire to fight for us when something went wrong.

I had bought plane tickets over a month before to go and visit him in San Francisco. My inability to maintain any type of composure was exposed through those gut-wrenching sobs, which were as uncontrollable as waves crashing against the shore. They just kept coming. Miraculously, in the end, there was a complete turnaround. It seemed that Fernando had decided that I should not have been put through this, and he had been feeling jealous (though I had no inkling what was wrong before he shared this fact with me). From this incident, I realized how important it was for us to be able to communicate our feelings openly and honestly in order to avoid any similar future misunderstandings. We ended off the conversation with I love you's, and my heart was again at ease - well, mostly.

After this discussion, I walked into Colleen's living room where she looked at me and immediately asked, "Have you been crying?" My eyes were so puffy and swollen; there would have been no way to conceal my pitiful condition. I revealed the bare bones story to her, and after hanging out a bit, I went to bed shell shocked and worried.

Although everything had been "sorted out" between Fernando and me, there was that sick feeling in the back of my mind that maybe everything was NOT ok. For him to wave the white flag of surrender for no logical reason, and to admit defeat in our relationship so effortlessly, was alarming. What I was trying to decipher now was, were things shaky for him now, or for me?

Throughout the weeks that followed the fall-out of that night, our relationship remained intact and strong. No other land mines exploded, shaking our foundation. At the end of September, as planned, I flew out to California to see my man! From the moment my plane landed, until he was hugging me goodbye, the weekend was perfect in every way. Wandering the streets, visiting quaint stores, and chatting about everything under the sun, we continued to bond.

We spent Saturday afternoon soaking up the sun at the beach, people watching, and discussing dreams and future plans. Cuddled up, I am sure people saw us as the poster children for "perfect couple". And I am not going to lie, I felt like we went together like peanut butter and jelly.

On our way out of San Francisco, we came across an incredibly beautiful park nestled right by the ocean. Fernando glanced over at me with a question mark in his eyes, and immediately I declared, "We have to go explore that place!" In less than an hour the sun would set, so we had limited time to bask in the breathtaking beauty around us. For a girl trapped in the desert ten months out of the year, the views were indescribable. Taking countless pictures of ourselves, the sunset, and the scenery, we basked in the knowledge of how lucky we were to have found each other. When we were inevitably torn apart by distance again, we knew we would be able to look back at these snap shops, on this perfect evening, and remember our reasons for enduring the struggle of a long distance relationship.

As the weekend wrapped up with a trip to Fernando's church on Sunday, and then returning to the airport, I remember feeling a tremendous amount of gratitude. Both of us had shared, more than once during this trip, how perfect our time together had been. It had, without a doubt, been the perfect combination of romance and friendship. As Fernando held my hand at the airport, I felt that I had finally found "the one". This was my happy ending! Sure, it had been a long time coming, and there had been many dates I'd suffered through to reach this point, but finally the effort had paid off. I had found the man with whom I wanted to dream, laugh, and create a life.

Or so I thought. Never in my wildest nightmare could I have envisioned what would occur less than a month later, after this cozy trip to California. After an unusually hectic week at school, the bomb dropped. Even though I was tired and worn out, I'd made time every night to speak to Fernando right before I went to bed.

On one particularly hectic day, I woke up late, and there was no time to even check my Facebook page before tearing out of my house to make it to school on time. At lunch when I finally had a moment to breathe, I had opened up my Facebook account to discover that Fernando had left me a message he had written the night before:

```
Karen,

I'm tired of all this. That simple. I think your work takes
everything from you. I have tried to be patient but I think
the real facts must be faced. Your work demands all of you,
and there is nothing left for a relationship. I have the
right to say, There is not room for a man in your life. The
distance make things hard, but the type of work you have
makes it impossible. I can't continue with this, it's
nonsense to me.

Is all I want to say,
```

There were students working on late assignments in my room at the time when I read this disturbing email, and I suddenly felt as if Francisco had just kicked me in the kneecap. The pain was paralyzing. Wait a minute! When I had texted him good morning like I always did before school, he had texted me back, as if all was well. My heart started to pound, and I couldn't help but feel trapped in my classroom. Eyes welling up, I told my students I would return as quickly as possible. Barely glancing up from their books, they continued reading, as I snatched up my cell phone and made a break for it. This was crazy! What in the world was happening? Immediately dialing Fernando's number, I was ridiculed by his answering machine message. Once I had left a voice mail, I saw that I had received a text. Sure enough, it was from him.

The following is the cold and upsetting text conversation that left such an ache in my heart, that I almost completely lost it:

F: Can't talk right now

K: You sent me the worst message on Facebook that I could imagine! I am beyond upset. You must feel no love for me at all. You have made me feel like a complete fool! THANKS A LOT!

F: You make your own conclusions. It's what I think and feel.

K: You are a coward to not say anything to me at all and then write that. I bet you met someone else and this is an excuse to dump me.

F: Just ask yourself for a few seconds how I feel! Thanks a lot!

K: You break up with me via Facebook and want sympathy?

F: I wrote that message half an hour after you went to bed. I'm not a coward (but again make your own conclusions). I have not met someone else.

K: Fine. I guess this is goodbye.

F: We can talk after work if you want.

Now I had moved outside my classroom, behind the school building. Students did not hang out or play sports there during lunch, so no curious eyes were wondering why Miss Rissling looked as if she was going to burst a blood vessel in her forehead. Not knowing what else to do, I called up one of my best friends, Jenn. Ring. Ring. Ring. Each second felt like an eternity. While I was not expecting her to answer her phone due to work, relief washed over me when I heard her voice.

"Hey Karen, how are you?"

"Not very good," I replied as the tears started to flow freely down my cheeks.

"Hey! What's wrong? Did something happen?"

"I think Fernando and I broke up," I replied, my voice cracking.

"WHAT?!?!"

I cannot remember any more of the conversation than this, because I was crying too hard and just trying to listen to Jenn's murmured reassurances. The advice she gave me was to ask my principal if there was someone who could cover my last class, so I could leave. This was a wise idea, as I was in no condition to be around children.

After miraculously cornering my extremely busy boss in the library, and briefly explaining my ordeal, I was told not to worry about anything, but to go ahead and leave. My class would be taken care of. There is nothing like crying in front of your principal to humble you. Fortunately, she is also one who has been known to shed a tear or two at times, and is typically very reasonable and understanding.

Immediately hightailing it to my friend Jenn's house, I felt that my relationship with Fernando had ended. The initial shock had started to wear off, and it was being replaced by a freezing over of my heart and emotions. Was this mean and cruel man the same person with whom I had envisioned spending the rest of my life? Telling a friend the details made it even more real, and I just sat hugging my legs to my chest and crying. During the next hour or so, Jenn and I talked about the situation and prayed together. I felt some comfort. Or was that just the numbing of my insides? Jenn suggested that Fernando's email may have been a plea for attention. Even so, I had concluded that if he would handle a problem with me in such a ruthless way, an important flaw of his character was being revealed. Later that afternoon he tried to contact me:

```
F:   Hey Karen

K:   I left (work)

F:   Everything is about you...that's the problem. But if you want
     to talk, just let me know.

K:   You are the one who called our relationship nonsense.

F:   Your job is your everything, your boyfriend, you, your
     God…..THATS nonsense to me.

K:   Work is my God?  Where in the world did you come up with
     something like that?  Well it sounds like you think I'm not
     even a Christian. Good thing Jesus knows my heart.

F:   What I mean is: your job absorbs everything from you. It's
     not being easy for me neither. ☹
```

After this text conversation, I refused to take his call an hour later. He then left me a message asking me to contact him. As the evening continued, I wondered if it wouldn't just be better to touch the pot I knew was hot in order to get this unpleasant conversation over and done with.

Fernando picked up the phone right away when I called. He stuck to his guns that he was right in feeling neglected, and how I was inconsiderate of his feelings. Apparently during our last few conversations, I had yawned into the phone, which made him feel like "a piece of crap". While I could see his side of things, I had tried to call him earlier one of the nights to which he was referring, only to be told he was having coffee with a friend and we could continue the conversation later. It seemed that Fernando could easily identify the times he perceived me as inconsiderate, but was unable to see himself in that same light.

Explaining my point of view, and accepting Fernando's feelings of being ignored and dismissed, we came to the agreement that we should be more considerate of each other. In spite of the fact that we ended the phone call on a positive note, part of me wondered if this was just a bump in the road, leading to a downhill slide over the side of a ravine.

The next night, I made the conscious effort to call Fernando early in the evening, so that he would feel that he had captured my full attention. I wanted to ensure that he felt appreciated and important. Not long into the call, he suddenly told me he had to get off the phone and he would call me back. Although I had made plans with a friend that evening, I cancelled them just in case Fernando would interpret this as another snub, dredging up all the difficulties of the day before. "Better safe than sorry," I thought, as I called off my get together. That night I never heard back from him. In the morning, by text, I did mention that I had waited for him to call me. I got the token sorry, and decided to let it go.

All afternoon Fernando texted me and told me he loved and missed me. When I asked him if he had bought the ticket to come visit, he avoided giving me a straight answer. This was perfect foreshadowing to what was to take place the following day. After a lengthy two hour phone call, where I was told how beautiful and wonderful I was, in a million years, I would never have guessed just how ugly things were going to get.

Before church on Sunday morning, I sent a message to Fernando wishing him good morning. He replied to my text, but by that time, church services had already begun. My phone was on silent mode. Sitting with my friend Sharon, I glanced down and noticed that my Blackberry's red light was flashing. It was then I saw that I had received a 2-part text from Fernando. With a sense of dread, my heart started to hammer as I read them:

```
F:   At home still…Karen, find strength in the Lord, he must be
     the first in your life…I want to tell you this today…you are
     not in school and you can find strength in the church….I
     cannot continue in this relationship.

F:   Of course I'm planning to call you to talk about it. Did you
     get/read my previous messages?
```

Wait a minute. Am I missing something here? Wasn't this man sending me "kissy muuuuuuuahhhh" texts less than 10 hours ago? Now he had decided that it was a good idea for him to break up with me while I was in church? This was definitely hitting below the belt!

Not able to sit and focus on anything but trying to figure out what had just happened; I stepped outside and attempted to call him. I must have misunderstood the text. The Fernando I knew who had held my hand on the beach would never pull a stunt like this. He picked up the phone and really didn't give me any solid answers to my myriad of questions. Instead, what seemed like the sorriest excuses he could come up with poured out of his mouth.

Needing to retrieve my things from the church, I quietly slipped into the sanctuary where my friend Sharon was sitting. She saw how upset I was, and left with me to talk and pray about what had happened. She felt very strongly that God was letting me know what could lie ahead in a relationship with Fernando, and that it would be up to me to make the choice of whether or not I wanted to be with him. At first, I did not understand how I even had an option, seeing how he had already abruptly broken up with me. Later I would see it. It wouldn't be long, even though the worst of the storm was yet to hit.

I still remember that it was unusually warm and sunny for October. After returning home to my empty apartment, alone with my thoughts, the texts from Fernando started to pile up in my inbox. "We need to talk. Call me." "We need closure." "I want to hash things out." I dreaded this particular conversation, but by mid afternoon, I knew it was time to get it over with.

Feeling the warmth of the sun on my face did nothing to thaw the ice on my heart. The hurt I had now morphed into fury. "Better to talk to him now," I thought, "while I am angry at him."

He picked up on the fourth ring. Probably a power play to make me wait for him. I found myself with very little to say, which was fine, since Fernando had several issues he wanted to bring up. I was told that if I would be open to receiving the constructive criticism that he was offering, that I could truly grow in my personality and character. How caring and selfless of him to take time out of his busy schedule to counsel me! Arrogant jerk. In total, there were three morsels of wisdom that he would present me with.

The first point he made was that he felt that I was showing him off on my Facebook account like a male trophy. Really? That is a pretty high opinion you have of yourself, Fernando! Did he really think that I felt more important or that my friends would love or like me more because I had a boyfriend? When I started to dispute this point, he interrupted me to ask if I could just let him continue.

Point two. This egotistical idiot stated the fact that I had drastically changed my behavior to try to make him feel loved and respected; that I was only doing things to "please him". This was in relation to the late night phone calls, where he felt that he was getting the last crumbs of my time. What a horrible girlfriend I was for listening to his concerns, and then proactively working on the behavior that was causing him pain! There was no winning in this situation. If I had not changed my behavior, then I was continuing to be disrespectful. If I did, then I was a wishy-washy people pleaser! After he told me this, I did stand my ground and debated this issue with him. It felt like he ignored everything I said, dismissing every word out of my mouth as being "defensive".

The third and final judgment that Fernando bestowed upon me was that he said my relationship with God was not up to snuff, as he had hoped it would be. After all, he had gone on a Christian website hoping to meet a "dedicated" Christian woman, not just someone that goes to church on Sundays. Now, I am sometimes just as distracted and busy as the next believer, but I love Jesus. Anyone who really knows me would never question that! Unless I am delusional, I believe that my life also reflects this passion. A purposefully hurtful comment like this, from someone who had claimed to love me, cut me down at the knees. Sitting on the hot pavement, I had lost my desire to even grace all of these attacks on my character with any explanations. He wasn't worth the effort or exertion. In an instant, the defiance evolved into resignation. Completely deflated and emotionally drained, I called a few friends, and debriefed everything that had happened that day.

As it turns out, Sharon was right. As early as that evening, Fernando began to send me texts declaring how much he loved and missed me. He proclaimed that he had made the biggest mistake of his life when he had acted so irrationally. He begged me to speak to him on the phone. I refused. Despite his promises that he would never intentionally hurt me again, I no longer felt emotionally safe with this man, and wanted to cease contact with him. He tried to rationalize his behavior, convince me of his unwavering love, but he never once admitted that the way he treated me was wrong.

Although we had officially broken up on October 10th, he continued actively trying to win me over up until the middle of November. Part of me believed that there was a miniscule chance that we could reconcile, so until

December, I still felt that I was "part of a couple" (even though it was clearly a dysfunctional relationship headed for certain doom).

After hearing about what happened, my friends and family couldn't stand Fernando. They still think he was like the old nasty gum that gets stuck to the bottom of your shoe. Hard to get rid of and irritating. Even if he could have made it up to me, how could I justify to my loved ones getting back together with someone who had treated me so horribly?

A month after our official break up, I spent a weekend with good friends at the International House of Prayer, in an effort to seriously consider what life with someone who could turn on me in a minute, would be like. After prayer and meditation, I came to the final realization that a relationship with Fernando was an unattainable dream. Good council from friends and family solidified my decision, and I dreaded having to deal with the emotional explosion that I was sure would ensue when I returned to El Paso.

As it turns out, even though Fernando had pleaded with me to call him as soon as I came home from this mini retreat, I have not heard a peep from him since. No emails. No texts. No phone calls. No surprise visits (which he had alluded to). I believe that means he saw the same thing I did. Even though I know that this was the best case scenario; Fernando had simply moved on, a part of me still felt the lingering loss accompanied by an overriding relief.

After Fernando's many attempts to win me back, he finally gave up. People always ask me how he could so quickly change from a perfect boyfriend to an irrational mad man. There are a lot of details that I am barely mentioning - from Fernando writing my mother messages on Facebook defaming my character, to sending a vindictive and provocative email to one of my best friends in Canada. I suspect from a previous conversation we had in passing a few months before, that there were some mental health issues involved in his sudden behavior changes. I'm not a psychiatrist, so I will refrain from providing a diagnosis.

There are no hard feelings anymore. Whatever Fernando was going through, I am grateful that our relationship did not continue, so the messes of meeting my parents or a broken engagement were avoided!

I want to apologize to my reader, who was probably assuming from the misleading title of this chapter, that the "happily ever after" ending that he or she is striving toward was not proven in this account. (Though the question mark in the title probably forewarned you) If things had ended differently, you could have shown your friends this book and gloated, "See, this woman was between the ages of 35 and 45 and was able to find her dream man online. Surely that is possible for me as well."

Don't feel sorry for me, as my journey is not over. I do still hold onto some joyful memories with Fernando, and I choose to still treasure those. Once the wounds began to heal, I would eventually (against some friends' advisements) go online once more to see if the perfect person for me is within reach of a mouse click. I have heard some single people call dating a "numbers game". I have heard the saying that we have to "kiss a lot of frogs" to get to our prince. Ultimately though, I believe looking for love is a journey that needs to be enjoyed. I am happy. I am single. Though at times it may seem that these two ideas cannot be compatibly connected, at the end of the day I can say that I am a happy single woman. One who plans to live her life to the fullest until the right man comes alongside me, and we discover that maybe, just maybe, we can merge together as partners. Your own dating outlook might seem bleak now, but remember that everything can change in an instant. I found God to be a source of peace and contentment throughout the Fernando situation, and that helped me to pick myself up, dust myself off, and move forward.

Post Fernando Online Dating

ALRIGHT, LET'S RECAP. I know a lot of you were bitterly disappointed that the Fernando fairytale never came to fruition, none of you more so than me. This book is not a present that has been neatly wrapped and tied up with a bow, meant to let you, the reader know that "he is out there". I, myself, am still trying to figure out if this is possible.

When I allowed Fernando to read parts of this memoir while visiting him in California, he kissed me and assured me that it was going to be a huge hit, and I would have no problem publishing it. When we broke up and I refused to take him back, he then immediately switched gears, and in an angry email informed me that he felt that this book would only hurt people's feelings because he thought it poked fun at them. I now see that this statement was merely the rejection talking. He wanted to know if he was just another "chapter in my book". At the time I had no idea that he meant literally, not figuratively. He had known that he had "made it into the book", albeit with a name change, and was worried that his cameo would not be a flattering one. He was partially right.

As mentioned earlier, I loved the person he was until everything went south. There were times I thought it would be impossible for me to feel happier or more comfortable with anyone else. If he chooses to read this, I hope he doesn't skip this part or think I am being sarcastic. It is tragic and heartbreaking that our relationship didn't work out, but it is what it is.

Wherever he is, I wish him well.

After spending time over Christmas break with my family and emotionally regrouping, I felt it was time to march back into the ring. (Without wearing the mini-skirt and thigh high boots the Wrestler wanted me to be decked out in) The longer I put off dating, the harder it would be. Trust me when I say that in no way had I missed the online dating rat race! Do you know how much time I saved not having to look through profiles, wink back at prospects, and create witty emails for men I don't know? Enough to write a chunk of this book, that's how much!

I had more than enough stories to complete this book, and probably a sufficient amount to create a sequel. This project was not the reason for me to start dating again.

Deciding that I had to be proactive in getting back out on the dating scene again, I decided to sign back up with Match.com. I knew that meeting some local gentlemen would be a way to get to know people quickly and intimately. Perhaps I wouldn't be surprised by extreme behavior, the way I had been with Fernando, if I could get to know someone via a more day-to-day, face-to-face regular life experience. Grudgingly, I went ahead and signed up for a few months. Short of a miracle, I did not see any upcoming opportunities in which I would meet eligible man within my social/career circles, and so I knew I needed to push myself, and make myself open to the possibility of romance again.

Love had to be just around the corner now, after all that I had invested in this quest. My memories of hikes on survival wilderness weekends remind me that just when you want to quit because you feel weak and tired, that spectacular view is likely just around the next bend. Here are some my dating experiences post Francisco.

·········;=)

OMG Guy

> Unfortunately, once he opened his mouth, it was all downhill from there. Suddenly the jeep wasn't so rugged; it was mud-splashed and dirty. After viewing the lab's pictures on his iPhone, the dog looked unkempt, scruffy, and like it might have rabies. Not to mention I was starting to wish that his English wasn't so effortless.

Halfheartedly, I started to look at profiles of gentlemen who had viewed my profile, and scanned over the new winks and emails I had received. The previous summer it had been nearly decadent not to even have to consider "shopping for guys". Now I had come full circle. I was back in the ring for round two. I could almost hear the bell striking. DING DING DING.

There was one man, Daniel, who stood out because he actually mentioned in the first line of his profile that he loved God. He had eyes that smiled merrily and a big grin in his picture, so I felt that he would be the perfect candidate for my first "post serious relationship" date. Following several breezy emails, Daniel asked me out. Unfortunately, I was on my way out of town that weekend, so we tentatively planned to meet the following Saturday.

He emailed me late in the week to tell me he would text me Saturday morning to set things up. When I did finally receive his text on Saturday around noon, I was already close to calling off our meeting to spend the day watching Gilmore Girls, while sorting through the mountain of papers and receipts that taunted me in my living room and kitchen. Throughout the string of text messages, I began to get a nagging feeling that Daniel had a vastly different sense of humor from my own, but I shunned the thought almost immediately, simply blaming nerves.

We decided to meet at Starbucks for coffee around 2:30 pm. This seemed the less intimidating choice, and at least I knew I would be able to make a quick getaway if necessary, unlike a dinner date or special event. Of course, I had to carefully consider at which Starbucks we should rendezvous. It couldn't be one of the cafes I most frequented, as it would be odd for me to take him where the baristas recognized me. Please note the repetition of this idea of not "dating" where you "drink your coffee", and you will thank me later!

I also do a lot of my writing at these locales. Trying to put pen to paper at home is not always a successful venture when your laundry and dishes are staring you down, sternly demanding your time and attention. I didn't want a bad online date to ruin my favorite "home away from home", especially since the lovely people there had, by now, learned to successfully concoct delicious skinny lattes specifically to my liking.

I chose a Starbucks on the other side of town. Arriving on time, I knew Daniel would be hanging out in the parking lot, as indicated in his most recent text. I confidently sauntered up to him, grinned, and gave him a hello hug. Regardless of whether we'd ever saw each other again; I have found that if I do not find the blind date repulsive, it is a great ice breaker to engage in a quick "friend" - type embrace. Let me comment that "on paper" Daniel was fantastic! He had a rugged green jeep, a house, a yellow lab (my very favorite dog), was a Christian, looked like his picture, had a job, was over the age of 25, and spoke English fluently.

Unfortunately, once he opened his mouth, it was all downhill from there. Suddenly the jeep wasn't so rugged; it was mud-splashed and dirty. After viewing the lab's pictures on his iPhone, the dog looked unkempt, scruffy, and like it might have rabies. Not to mention I was starting to wish that his English wasn't so effortless.

I feel almost cruel even stating these observations, especially since he had eagerly purchased my overpriced latté. You know how we girls sometimes rummage half-heartedly through our purses, as if we are frantically searching for our own debit cards, waiting for the guy to offer to foot the bill? In my defense I did offer to pay, and even pulled out my wallet with true intent to do so.

Within minutes of ordering our lattés and sitting down at a table outside, I could already see that although he was a very congenial person, I was not feeling a personality connection at all.

The first annoyance was how he made SUCH a huge deal out of the fact that I am Canadian. All the clichéd jokes were touched on. From how much we love our maple leaves to how we still live in igloos. He may have thought he invented all these clever stereotypes, but I already owned a novelty T-shirt containing a list of these, and many more. Of course he also had to mention how we "talk funny". Trying to be comical, he started adding the famous Canadian word "eh" onto the end of every sentence he uttered. It stopped being funny after the first two phrases, and then I was becoming embarrassed for him.

That combined with the "OMG's" that just kept coming, finished off any potential chemistry for me, securing Daniel a place in the friend zone. OMG is something that my seventh grade girls may say, but that the boys would never even dare murmur, unless they said it in a falsetto girl's voice. A phrase like this does not in any way fit a 40 year old man with muscular arms and a tight black shirt. For a fleeting moment, the thought that we could be friends ran through my mind. Realistically, even if he said he was open to the idea, a guy who is online looking for love is usually not looking for another friend.

After being held voluntarily captive for almost two hours, I was ready to make a break for it. A text came in from one of my best friends, and I jumped at the chance to head for the hills. Of course, the most awkward part of an artificial or blind date like this is when you decide to part ways. What does one say to someone you know will probably never again cross your path? "Take care." "Great to meet you." "Keep in touch." Something trite. And no matter how hard you try, it always comes out feeling shallow and insincere.

With haste, and an overwhelming hankering for a passion tea, I headed to my real hangout, a neighborhood Starbucks close to home, to debrief this meeting with Colleen, my adoptive little sister. The only thing that could have been worse about the date through which I had just suffered, would have been if he had been one of the Starbuck Baristas at my regular refueling coffee shop. This caffeinated connoisseur, who I have grown to respect only for his extreme passion for coffee, shamelessly shares his infinite wisdom about the creation and perfection of his drink concoctions in an effort to try to pick up female customers. Any chance he gets.

After recapping date particulars with Colleen, we overheard him as he went into explicit detail about one beverage, specifically targeting the bubbles, how they were shaped, and how they should look. This was done in order to impress two cute 20-somethings. My friend and I timed his ranting about this coffee creation, without taking a breath, for a full 90 seconds. Insert here the polite laughter of the girls trapped in this tirade. Next, insert the belly laughs of Colleen and me as we observed this ridiculous scene unfold.

As silly as it may sound, this was just what the doctor had ordered to lighten my spirit after yet another unsuccessful date; unfortunately, my first after the end of a serious relationship.

When I'd left Starbucks to head home, part of me wondered if I still had the heart and stamina to continue the quest of online dating. You almost have to be as pugnacious as a dog that has one end of a sock and persistently keeps tugging and tugging, hoping that his master will eventually tire of the game and release the prized possession. Would my treasured sock ever materialize? The more stories I heard from single women, the more I wondered.

Four months before I would have sworn that finding love on the Internet was possible, but my faith was wavering. Faith. Shouldn't my faith be in God alone to provide that person for me? Yet God helps those who help themselves right? I know it wasn't realistic to imagine I could meet Mr. Right so soon after re-entering the dating scene. Would I have to go on two more dates? Ten? Ten thousand? (I know I am being dramatic). The next few months would prove to be out of the ordinary, and provide me with a chance to head out of my comfort zone!

.... ;=)

Let's Talk Babies!

> On one hand, he had already told me that he'd felt a strong physical attraction for me. On the other hand, he'd already had visions of babies sitting on his lap, calling him, "Da da", and decking himself out with tacky **WORLD'S GREATEST DAD** t-shirts.

One gentleman found me on Match.com, and made it very clear that he was interested in getting to know me right away. Immediately after seeing that he was 33 years old, I dropped the 40 year old bomb on him (remember how I explained earlier how I was unable to change my age on my profile?). His almost instant return email to me stated that age did not matter, and then commenced by asking me several questions. I, in turn, shot some inquiries his way.

His last email to me was short and sweet. "Do you see yourself with children? Do you want them?"

Back to reality. This bachelor in his 30's was looking for a baby maker. I wondered if he was friends with Tim (from the Chapter 3). I replied that I was up for whatever God wanted, but I also knew the risks for a woman over 35 when looking to give birth were legitimate and serious.

My Match.com inbox remained empty for several days. Part of me figured that a guy so direct about kids, so quickly, was really just looking to procreate. I imagined a cartoon-shaped hole as a result of him bursting through the wall in his haste to retreat after he read my email. Then, I received a response which let me know what had happened:

> Hi, Made it back into town. I was out of town on business. Let's talk about the kid thing some more. I know what you mean about waiting until you get married to have children...then it doesn't happen. God always has a plan!

Wow…..This guy was already dreaming of his first bambino. I saw how conflicted he was. On one hand, he had already told me that he'd felt a strong physical attraction to me. On the other hand, he'd already had visions of babies sitting on his lap, calling him, "Da da", and decking himself out with tacky *WORLD'S GREATEST DAD* t-shirts.

What ended up being disconcerting for me was that he'd come off sounding like he was feeling sorry for me. He had thrown me a bone at the end, by reminding me that God had a plan. Sigh. Part of me wanted to inform him that not every woman in the world was yearning to give birth. No need to pity me, Padre. My niece and nephew, otherwise known as "Mamacita" and "Jefé" (little mama and boss in Spanish) have always been the apples of my eye. I'd enjoyed spoiling them, playing, and chatting with them. It would be hard to imagine having my own kids at this point, and maybe adoption would be an alternative I would consider if God led me in that direction. For now, I was content with my current situation.

Having this stranger inform me that he wanted to "talk about this kid thing some more" made me wonder why he hadn't asked me any personal questions about my preferences, goals, hobbies, family (the one I already had), or friends. It felt like he just didn't want to invest the time if he didn't have the guarantee of offspring as a possibility. That was a huge turn off!

There is so much more to me than being a potential mother. I am a teacher, a daughter, an aunt, a friend, and a sister. Is it demented that I had partially wanted to reply just to see what he would do? Unfortunately, I have Pandora-like tendencies and desire to lift up the lid, even knowing that mayhem will probably result. In the end, I decided to leave the lid on. After all, curiosity killed the cat, or in this case, may have killed my desire to continue meeting men online.

.... ;-)

Cougar Chronicles

I am not trying to fib about my age, hoping to rope myself a young stallion. I found myself in the role of the reluctant cougar, not by choice, but by circumstances.

Apparently I have run out of eligible men my own age to date in El Paso. It was bound to happen eventually, but it occurred, almost without warning, sneaking up on me like a devious cat pouncing on a clueless mouse.

On a free dating site I frequented, the mail that I was receiving had come from a different age demographic than had been previously contacting me. Having recently posted some new pictures of myself with my darker hair, perhaps this was the draw for some of these new young bucks.

Checking my email, I would see a new message had come in, and it became my automatic reaction to immediately scroll down the profile after a quick peek at the guy's face (I am a face girl), to see his age. At this point, I would hold my breath, hoping that the guy was at least 30 years old, and under 55 years old. On this particular website, my age is clearly stated. 40 year old woman. There is no mystery. I am not trying to fib about my age, hoping to rope myself a young stallion. I found myself in the role of the reluctant cougar, not by choice, but by circumstance.

.... ;-)

Javier: the Unexpected

Less than five minutes into our conversation, he had already told me about a "Snuggy" party to which he had been invited. No, I am not kidding.

Constantly being told that you are a young 40 is flattering, but it doesn't change the fact that I am 40 and that is reality.

In this instance, on Match.com I had received a wink from an attractive 26 year old military man. He had reminded me of my first serious boyfriend, Mark. This makes perfect sense since Mark was 26 when we had broken up in the 90's. Had I really reverted back to dating the same aged men as I did when I was 21?

On a whim, I winked back, only to be sent the following email from a blunt and no nonsense Javier, "Since we have winked at each other, we should just go out on a date, since that is the reason we joined this website, right?" Not one to beat around the bush! I remember laughing out loud after reading the message, thinking that this guy had "cojones".

Unfortunately, we had started communicating right before I went home for Christmas over the break, so an impromptu meeting was impossible. He decided to call me while I was in Seattle, waiting for a shuttle to carry me toward the Canadian border. I wasn't sure if it was the connection or not, but he seemed to talk a million miles an hour, and it was hard to follow his train of thought. Part of me assumed that the connection wasn't the best, the other part wondered if this guy was just a hot mess. After occasional calls and very random (often one word) texts for the next month or so, we finally met at Barnes and Noble for a coffee date.

I know I am about to irritate a lot of men who are vertically challenged with a question that is on my mind. Why is it that many of these males will write on their profiles that they are 5'9"? After discussing this with Torri, one of my favorite colleagues from school, we came to our own conclusion that this is the "go to height" that men post or quote, even when it is CLEAR that they are not. Torri is 5'8" and has noticed this throughout her life. Men will proclaim, in all seriousness, that they are 5'9", but she usually has at least 2 inches on them.

Javier, a self proclaimed 5'9" gentleman, met me in front of the café. I am 5'6" and was wearing boots that likely put me at 5'8". He was noticeably shorter than me, in fact I felt like I should be a giant green man advertising vegetables on television commercials.

Usually when I meet someone new, I can tell whether or not there is a spark of interest in his eyes. I have the uncanny ability to discern if there is attraction or not right off the bat. From Javier I was receiving absolutely NO signal that I appealed to him at all. Less than five minutes into our conversation, he had already told me about a "Snuggy" party to which he had been invited. No, I am not kidding. I am referring to those cheesy, static-laden blankets with sleeves, which were all the rage on the commercials a few years back.

This fiesta was one in which each person had to bring his or her own individual Snuggy to wear. Although I cannot say with absolute certainty, I would also guess that an abundance of alcohol would be consumed at this shindig. (Probably to avoid acknowledging the pain from the static shocks having to be endured from all of those Snuggies in one place) I mean, if wearing Snuggies was all this party was about, there had better be some kind of compensation to block out the embarrassment of adorning these garments. After hearing about his plans, I think I felt about a hundred years old. It made my plans of hanging out with a friend, sound like I was over the hill and no fun. Or sane.

When a guy immediately mentions what he is going to do after his time with you is up, this would indicate, to me at least, that he has no intention of getting to know you. Usually I feel that I can keep a man's attention, and be entertaining on a date. With this guy, I felt like I was sitting with a hyperactive 7th grader who had not been given his daily dose of Ritalin for a week. Combine with this the constant checking of his cell phone, and it was all I could do to be polite and make small talk.

Finally escaping under the pretext that I was going to be late to my pressing engagement, (yeah right), I took a deep breath, got into my car, and almost peeled out of there.

So you can imagine my shock when 5 days later, I received a text from Javier during one of our rare snow days off from school. There had been rolling power outages to conserve on the skimpy amount of electricity the city had available, and many people had been left without heat and power in their homes. El Pasoans are wimpy when it comes to the cold, and in all fairness, do not know how to prepare or deal with frigid weather conditions. The city becomes paralyzed when there is even a threat of freezing temperatures or a dusting of snow. Midwestern towns mock us, but we can't help it. We just don't handle winter adversity well.

So despite the rumors and multiple Facebook updates about power outages, mostly from enraged students who were no longer able to chat with their best friends for hours online, I had not yet been directly affected by this "storm". At first, I'd stuck close to home as this was what all the solemn, deep-voiced newscasters had strongly suggested. El Paso Storm Watch 2011 monopolized the news channels, and finally at around 2pm I decided to venture out into the "winter wonderland" to feed my addiction to skinny cinnamon dolce lattes from Starbucks.

Knowing that my writing conference in New York was quickly approaching, and that my manuscript for this book wasn't going to write itself, I had decided to dedicate at least an hour and a half to writing another chapter that had been on my mind. In fact, ironically, it was about the boys, yes I said it - boys, I had recently been meeting online.

Suddenly, an annoying chirp from my phone informed me that a text had come in. I figured it was from either a friend telling me about another possible snow day, or from Ben, the other young man I had been out on a few dates with (more on him later). Shock slapped me across the face when I saw that it was JAVIER who had sent me a text. Really? Are you kidding me? I would have readily bet a large sum of money that this guy was never going to appear in my life again.

His text, like most of the ones before I had met him, was the equivalent of a man grunt. "Hi". So I responded back, "Hi". The next text said, "Hey." Come on now. You started texting me buddy! Don't make me carry this "conversation", because I am currently busy writing about how I should probably give up dating younger men like you. You are only supporting my hypothesis with your monosyllabic responses.

After I had finished a lengthy phone conversation with a friend, I discovered that Javier had sent me a few back-to-back texts. Turns out that his power had gone out and he was really cold. It must have been out of desperation that he asked me, "Could you come over and keep me warm?" Rewind. This was a guy who had shown, in my opinion, absolutely no sexual attraction to me at all! Why in the world was he propositioning me? My burst of laughter caused the elderly man sitting in the comfy chair beside me to almost spill his Starbucks coffee. "Let's just see how this plays out," I thought to myself, so I replied to Javier's texts and told him he was welcome to come and hang out at my place, since my heater was working great. In fact, we could even watch movies, since a friend of mine, aka the other young man in my life, had brought over a mountain of DVDs for me to borrow.

I know what you might be thinking. Should I invite a strange guy into my home after a "not so successful" first date? My answer is probably not, but I did feel sorry for him. He was in the military, had no family in El Paso, and lived alone. Ask not what your country can do for you, but what you can do for your country right?

So I rushed home, tidied up a little, had a quick shower, and texted Javier to let him know he could come over when he was ready. Within an hour he arrived, and I was pleasantly surprised that he was much more polite and personable than when I had first met him. I genuinely enjoyed hanging out with him this time.

It was night and day compared to the Barnes and Noble fiasco. I do know I may have invited him over because I'd felt like Ben and I were becoming a little too close, and by being out with another man it felt like I was protecting my heart by not putting all my "eggs in one basket". Proudly, I showed him around the incredibly beautiful property on which I live, and he was impressed. In my apartment, he kept commenting on how cozy and inviting it was.

Once we started the movie, Javier was the perfect gentleman. He stayed on his side of the loveseat, which is small because my living room is miniscule. He still laughed and made comments, but was not overtly flirty with me. He thanked me at the end of the evening for letting him come over, and said that he had appreciated the refuge from his arctic apartment! Several times over the course of the evening I would look over at Javier, and felt more of a friendly fondness for him, rather than a romantic attraction.

The next day I met my friend, Nishna, at Barnes and Noble, and unexpectedly Javier came into the café to complete some work. Normally, I would have wondered if I'd looked ok or been a little frazzled, but instead I just walked over, and briefly greeted him on my way out. Maybe this was not a love connection, but I am grateful that I did hang out with him a second time, because I feel that we may still develop a positive platonic friendship. I learned that even if the first date is atrocious, if the guy wants a second chance, it might be in a girl's best interest to give him one.

·········· ;¬)

Ben: Young, But Surprisingly Old

> What would we talk about? Would we have anything in common? He'd been born a year before I'd graduated from high school. While the 80s had been a monumental fashion faux pas for me, he'd been in diapers for almost all of it.

Ben Abel Michael. The boy with three first names. When I'd told a few friends about going out with this fun new guy, one of the first things they would ask me for was his name. As soon as "Ben" slipped out of my mouth, they would flinch surprisingly and state, "Wow! That is a real 'white boy' name, Karen."

My disclaimer here is that my friends are <u>not</u> racists. Anyone who knows me is aware that I am one who tends to date men who are foreign, or who are of different ethnic backgrounds than my own Caucasian Euro-mix. I don't believe I do this intentionally, but my friends do tease me about it. I have dated exotic men from Puerto Rico, Haiti, Barbados, Peru, Venezuela, Columbia, Mexico, Dominican Republic, and India, just to list a few countries. So, when my friends are used to hearing names like Cesar, Angel,

Fernando, Raul, Ricardo, and Gustavo, Ben definitely stands out as being uniquely different from my dating norm.

Ben had written to me on a free dating website. As soon as I'd glanced at his age, I had no intention of replying. He was only 23 years old. Perhaps it was curiosity that had pushed me to read his email. It was one line, and it announced, "There is no way that you are 40!"

He'd sounded so optimistic about meeting, like it would be the most normal thing in the world. Maybe it was because he seemed so sweet, but I did write to him and pointed out the age difference, just in case he had perhaps missed it or thought I was joking. His reply was to "give him a chance".

Something about the simplicity of his request brought my guard down. We texted each other that whole day, since he was on 24-hour military duty. There was continued contact off and on again over the next few weeks. Finally, we'd decided that it would work to meet for afternoon coffee. At where else? Starbucks. Then we would hit a matinee at the theater nearby. True confessions here. I felt completely at ease when meeting Ben, simply because I was confident that we could not possibly be a good fit. I felt like a woman with nothing to lose.

Before you call me a pessimist, think about it. It is hard enough to connect with someone in your own age bracket, and here I was 17 years older than this young man. What would we talk about? Would we have anything in common? He'd been born a year before I'd graduated from high school. While the 80's had been a monumental fashion faux pas for me, he'd been in diapers for almost all of it. I think I've have made my point.

Once Ben showed up, I'd immediately noticed that he was one of those notorious 5'9" guys referenced earlier! For me though, height is not a deal breaker when it comes to boyfriend criteria. One of my best girlfriends will not even meet an online suitor unless he is at least 6 feet tall. She says if they state they are 6 feet, than there is at least a 90% chance they reach up to 5'10".

For me, the non-negotiable points to which I choose to cling lie more in the arena of illegal drug use, lack of a moral compass, and being married. Height is not an issue of character. If I could find a man who loved God, was honest, loyal, faithful, funny, and intelligent, and if there was an accompanying attraction there, it would not, in any way, matter about his height. I laugh at all those reality wedding shows out right now, where all the arrangements have to be extravagant! If I could find a man with all the above traits, I would be willing to marry him in a Wal-Mart parking lot.

We joked around and chatted outside, since every seat in the coffee shop was taken. In a way this felt more private, which I liked, and we were able to talk freely and laugh together.

I'd appreciated that Ben had been a gentleman, paying for my coffee and movie, and opening doors for me. Unfortunately, while we were waiting in the lobby, he was obligated to take calls from the soldiers he supervised. Half listening, but not wanting to be nosey, I heard him comment, "Come on! I am on a date here! You're killin' me!"

As I sat there waiting for him to finish his conversation, it suddenly occurred to me that I liked Ben. He seemed so real, so down to earth. In the almost completely deserted movie theater, I did feel an attraction for him that I was not expecting. When halfway through the movie Ben told me that I "made him nervous", I questioned him about that. His answer was revealing. This date with me was his first since his divorce. Part of me was flattered that he had felt I was worth the chance, but I could already predict the dating scene was going to be a tough arena for him to navigate.

Later that night while we were texting, I was teasing Ben about how he had been nervous at the movie, stating how I was the least intimidating person I know. He responded by saying that he was nervous because he wasn't sure if he should have tried to put his arm around me or hold my hand. I wondered if this was really how most guys felt, but were too macho or insecure to admit?

As the week went on, we continued texting, and by the following Friday, Ben had invited me out to a local watering hole with his friends. One of his fellow soldiers was shipping out to Iraq, and they were sending him off.

When I received his first text about the outing, I was out at a coffee shop with my "little sister", Colleen. With absolutely no intention of going, I offhandedly mentioned the invitation to her. She squealed and exclaimed, "We should totally go!" She was itching for a double date, which, as close friends, we had always wanted to experience together. Finally she had a boyfriend, and it looked like I was being asked on a second date!

"Colleen, I think it is a bad idea. What if all of his friends wonder why he would invite this ancient chick to come to this outing?"

"You are being silly. I will call Eddie and I say we go!" was her indignant reply. Then after a couple more convincing texts from Ben, my phone rang. His number. I picked up, only to find there was a girl on the other end of the line. She introduced herself as a girlfriend of one of Ben's buddies. Apparently she was leaving town the next day as well, said that she had heard a lot about me, and had wanted me to come down and meet everyone. Just the fact that Ben had gone to all the trouble of trying to make me feel that I was invited and welcome changed my mind, and I gave Colleen the two thumbs up. "But I need to go home and change clothes and freshen up my makeup," I insisted. Another squeal or two along with some bouncing on the couch cushions followed, and we drove back to my house to reapply eyeliner and search for a cute outfit, that was worthy of a fun night out.

I am not a woman who takes a long time to get ready, and so, when moments before we walked out the door, I received a text from Ben saying that they were leaving the bar, so I shouldn't come out, I was caught off guard. I'm not going to lie, I was fuming. I had pretty much rearranged my entire evening, as low key as it might have been, to accommodate Ben, at his insistent request. When I tried to call his cell, a guy answered and said he was in the restroom. Whatever.

"This is what I get," I thought, as I began to mentally beat myself up. Becoming hopeful too soon and opening myself up prematurely was a rookie mistake. Colleen had already called her boyfriend, so I told them to just go ahead and hang out. Even though she enthusiastically tried to persuade me to join them, at that point, I just wanted to put on my favorite sweats and read a mystery novel.

BEEP. BEEP. BEEP. I ignored the chirps alerting me to insistent apology texts I was receiving from Ben and went to bed. I disregarded the one I received in the morning as well, until I started to reflect on the fact that we had only been on one date. I needed to cut this boy some slack. I was treating him like he was my boyfriend, and I needed to relax and not be so demanding. Did I let him know that he had pretty much ruined my plans? Yes. Then I let it go.

As it turned out, he wanted to come over and watch movies that Sunday afternoon, which sounded good to me. Whenever a cute guy comes over, my apartment always gets a good cleaning. He arrived around 3pm, just as I had finished mopping the bathroom and kitchen floors. I was excited to see him, which also raised a question mark in my mind. He looked so cute, and he had brought over a mountain of DVDs that he wouldn't allow me to carry. All I wanted to do was kick back and relax with him.

Would he try to hold my hand or put his arm around me? After a debate concerning which movie to watch first, we compromised on a scary one with Samuel L. Jackson. He was one messed up, psychotic neighbor in this movie, which made it really engaging.

For the most part, during the first movie, Ben kept to his side of the loveseat. This was ok with me, because we were still having fun and flirting. It wasn't like I wanted him to pounce on me; after all, this was only a second date! The whole situation took me back to my high school/college days, where I recalled feeling that crush, not knowing for sure yet if it was reciprocated.

During our intermission, when I made him an egg white omelet, Ben did mention how thrilled his dad was that he had started dating a Christian girl. My ears perked up here. So we were dating? He had told his dad about us? Ok, but did he tell his dad that the girl in question was a forty year old woman? I actually asked him this, to which he responded that his parents wouldn't care. Yeah, right!

Next we watched <u>Anger Management</u> with Adam Sandler and Jack Nicholson. Great comedy. While laughing, suddenly Ben slid his arm around my shoulders. I put my head on his chest, and after a while he was holding my hand too. Girls, you know the difference between the cupping of the hand, and the fingers-intertwined hand holding. His fingers laced in mine like they had always been there. Ok, I realized that this is being a little over dramatic, but you have to realize that at this point I hadn't held hands with anyone since Francisco.

After the second movie, Ben got up to leave. I walked him out and he gave me a really long, drawn out hug. I liked that he hadn't made the move to kiss me yet, and felt that was because he must've really respected me. Later I would question my reasoning, due to the events that followed.

So after our Sunday cuddle fest, I guess I'd expected that Ben would be more prone to at least send me little texts, but to my surprise, I heard nothing from him the following Monday. You could hear the crickets chirping. The weird part was that I even sensed from early in the morning that he would not contact me. By about 6pm that night, I felt really shaken. The fact that I was reacting so strongly to Ben's lack of communication was actually a wake-up call for me.

Why did I care so much? We'd only gone on 2 dates, which did not a relationship make. Tuesday afternoon, the text came in from Ben to let me know that he had lost his phone, and he apologized for not being able to get in touch with me. Accepting this, but still uneasy, I noticed for the rest of the week that incoming texts were few and far between.

I'd even tried to invite him over during a snow day, but he'd said that he had been working a 24 hour shift and needed to go home and sleep. After being a little snippy with him, or how it surely sounded via text, I didn't hear from him for over 3 days.

In my frustration, I might have made the very blunt comment to Ben that I'd always hated getting "one word responses from my *guy friends*." Yes I actually threw the *friend* word out there. Ben does strike me as the sensitive type whose feelings could have been hurt by being positioned in the "friend zone". Or was I trying to concoct my own reasons, and generate my own excuses, for why he would lose interest in me?

I'd known that he was having a Super bowl party with "the guys" that Sunday, and the fact that he had made no effort to contact me, proved that I had once again let my hopes be raised too early. It was great to hear on Facebook that day that a good friend of mine had recently gotten engaged, ironically, to a military man she met on a dating site. I was happy for her, but frustrated for me. I'd probably done something wrong, at least that was the jilted girl's go to mantra right? If Ben had truly liked me and missed me, he would've wanted to see me, and that was the bottom line. Part of me wanted to text him, but I knew that was a self-destructive inkling.

After some serious thought, I have come to the conclusion that Ben was one of those men who'd wanted to be seen as a "good guy". He didn't want any girl to think he was a jerk for any reason at all. At first, this guy was into me, no doubt about it. However, somewhere along the relational path, he'd opted out. Now he was stuck with feeling that he'd stepped in a little too far, and didn't want to be the bad guy for changing his mind. If I'd decided to contact him, I was sure he would respond, but only out of obligation, because he wanted to be seen in a positive light. Let's face it; nothing can keep a man away from a woman in whom he is truly interested. He will make the time, go without sleep, be inconvenienced, and attempt ridiculous feats, just to be with her.

Ben had changed his mind, and I have no idea why. He'd started off strong, and then petered out. Now the pile of guy-themed DVDs on my living room floor ridiculed me, as they had convinced me that Ben wouldn't have brought over such a stash if he wasn't planning to stick around to watch them.

Suddenly, I recalled that his birthday was in four days. Should I text him "Happy Birthday", even if he had made no effort to contact me? The dilemma and social niceties to which I adhere would just be an excuse to contact him, and continue the self destructive cycle.

Ok. I caved. A moment of weakness. Every woman out there has done it. We knew we should not have texted the guy we had not heard from, but we went out on a limb and thought we would shoot off a breezy, casual message anyway. By this time, I had gone out with Juan (who I will discuss later), and felt that seeing him would soften any rejection I might feel if Ben chose to blatantly reject me. I was a woman with options. All my eggs were NOT in one basket!

After appealing to two of my best friends as to whether or not I should contact Ben, I heard two opposing opinions. Jenn, who is closer to my age, appealed to my sense of pride. "Don't do it," she argued, "Just wait until his birthday, and send him a text then."

On the other hand, Colleen had a different take on the situation. The fact that she is closer to Ben's age, and is much more versed in text etiquette for the younger sect, made me consider her viewpoint more carefully. "Karen, just send him a short text. If you did put the "friend" comment out there, then he needs to see that you are still interested in him as more than that. Just texting him a generic birthday text will not accomplish that task. The worst that can happen is he doesn't text back." So weakness or not, I sent a short text inquiring about the big Super bowl party he was throwing. His bosses' boss would be there, and he had felt pressure for it to be a memorable bash.

As it turned out, I received a text from Ben the day before his birthday. While at work, I'd had to run out and get lunch since I had forgotten mine at home, so we'd texted back and forth for the hour. During my prep period, I'd also called him to sing "Happy Birthday", since he was being so negative about turning 24. Yes, you heard me right. Ben was **devastated** about reaching this milestone.

At first I thought he was joking around, and then realized that he was genuinely upset. One part of me wanted to laugh, but I could tell that it would be inappropriate, so I controlled myself. Well, I held it in until he sputtered out, "At least next year when I turn 25, my insurance will go down a lot". Explosive laughter erupted, as I unsuccessfully attempted to cover the sound up with a cough-like noise. Had I reached an all time low in my dating adventures, when I was providing free phone therapy to a man almost half my age in how to deal with his impending birthday?

The phone call did provide me with some more information, that, as a woman, I fully intended to analyze to death. He'd seemed to like the fact that I was trying to cheer him up, and told me that it did make him feel special. Hmmmmmm. He'd also mentioned when I was making restaurant suggestions, that he'd wanted to take me for a date, but under no circumstances would he let me pay for us to eat there. Hmmmmmmm.

Then, the kicker was that Ben told me that he wanted to attend the Dave Ramsey course, for which I was registered at a local church. (He's a great financial advisor, if you've never heard of him) Not only did he wish to attend the one week where friends are invited, but he planned to continue for the entire duration. This gave me fodder to mull over and pick apart for several days. When I am not interested in a man, I do not devote this kind of attention to him. This made me feel very emotionally vulnerable, as I could see that I was starting to really like Ben.

This is where the longest dry spell of communication between us occurred. I did not hear from him on his actual birthday (a Wednesday), and the next time I'd received a text was on the Friday. The sentiment there was a simple, "I hate my job". Not sure how to respond to that statement, I replied with a sympathetically short, "I'm sorry.☹"

The weekend went by, and even in the embrace of another man (Juan), I still missed Ben. Valentine's Day came and went. Nothing. Out of all the men with whom I was communicating at the time, he was the one I wanted to hear from most.

Finally, the following Saturday, I got three back to back texts from Ben: "Karen!!!", "Yay! I got my new phone", and "Apple took forever, you probably thought I died. Lol." I almost did a cartwheel when I discovered he was back. And then of course, I messed things up. Once again I put my defensive walls up. I told him that because of the long bout of silence, I'd thought he didn't want to be friends with me anymore.

He then told me that I should call Apple and tell them how they made me lose communication with the coolest guy ever. I decided to call him (I still prefer phone calls to texts), and he sounded excited to chat. After awhile he did tell me he had another call, his pregnant sister, and had to go. That was at 11:30am. Not another peep out of him for the rest of the day or night. So, why did this man come on like gangbusters and then fizzle out flat like a 2 day old opened soda? For the record, that has to be the world's longest baby delivery, because I've never heard from Ben again. I think I will sell his DVD's to the highest pawn shop bidder, and use the cash to renew my membership on Match.com!

.... ;=)

The Random Two Weeks Of Men

Maybe I felt like I had nothing to lose by texting Ben because men seemed to have been coming out of the woodwork during the previous few weeks. As mentioned earlier, Javier came and hung out with me that Wednesday night. Even though it did not turn out to be a romantic date, it was still nice to be around an attractive young man, whose company I thoroughly enjoyed.

Throughout the week Doug, one of my first online flirtations, had been sending me Facebook messages, making references to my raspy voice and my attractive booty. On Friday night he took the initiative and called me from Korea, where he teaches English as a second language, "Karen, we need to see if we could meet somewhere when we both get a break from school. I just don't think we met by accident, and I still really like you." Before you start jumping up and down, wishing me well, I do have to forewarn you that Doug has been known to pop up sporadically, cast his charming web, and entangle me briefly. (See his story in Chapter 3) Then when he is confronted about acting on his claims of adoration, like a spider he scurries off into the unknown.

On Saturday, a 26 year old break dancer from a neighboring city contacted me, and even though I acknowledged that I was quite a bit older, I also remembered that I have always had a thing for guys who can dance, and have always found this genre to be the most fascinating. Even though he came on like a torrential rain, when I couldn't immediately meet up with him before his trip to LA, he disappeared like a puff of smoke. Since I had added him as a Facebook friend, I am reminded of him from time to time by the many notifications about B-Boy break dancing competitions. Not to mention that he also posts a lot of Youtube videos with songs that have extremely explicit lyrics, which leads me to think that we wouldn't have been a perfect match anyway. I will always have his updates.

The biggest surprise was the text I received on sunny Sunday afternoon. Juan Martinez, one of the few men featured in this book that I did not meet online, had contacted me. It had been about 6 months since we'd gone out on a date.

Now, how do I describe Juan? He is a very sexy guy. He is like a magnet that draws your gaze and attention right to him. His effortless charm draws you in. Add to that a drive to succeed, and he is a triple threat!

I first saw Juan in a class at the University of Texas El Paso. Seeing as my master's degree was in education, just the fact that there was an actual single man in the class was unusual. The girls would flock around him like moths to a flame. You couldn't blame them. Juan was intelligent, handsome, educated, and driven. These types of guys don't come around every day, and are a hot commodity in a city like El Paso. In the first class, Juan sat on the opposite side of the room, and I'd never had the opportunity to speak to him. My impression was that he seemed like a humble and down to earth guy and was likely married or taken, like every other decent man in town.

During the last semester of classes, I had signed up for a Scholarly Writing course, and lo and behold, who ended up sitting at my table? Juan. I'd like to think that it was my breathtaking beauty that made him choose his seat, but I know that the fact that our table was in the back, away from the watchful professor's eye and close to the exit, might actually have had more to do with his seating choice. As I spent more time with him during classes, I was able to add funny to his list of interesting attributes.

We got along well and had some decent conversations throughout the semester, but I was otherwise entangled with Brandon (an online suitor who ended up being a big waste of time). In a way, that was probably why it was comfortable for me to be friends with Juan. He'd asked me once if I'd ever dated people "casually". Being naïve, it took me awhile to realize he was hinting and trying to feel me out. He was really asking if I would have been willing to date him "casually". Though very flattered, and more than a little tempted, I refrained at that time. What was great about Juan was how he still made an effort to get to know me regardless.

We didn't become bosom buddies or hang out often, but there was enough of a personality connection that Juan visited my classes as a guest speaker, sharing his extensive knowledge of the Holocaust with my students (He was a history major with a concentration on World War II and Nazi Germany). Watching him challenge my students and present in such a dynamic way was extremely attractive. By this time, I had definitely recognized that we didn't want the same things when it came to the opposite sex - I wanted a relationship, Juan wanted a hook-up. We remained friends, another year went by, and he returned to speak to my classes once again, sharing his wealth of historical knowledge.

During that summer Juan had invited my dad and I to join him for dinner. My dad was in town to meet with immigration officials, as I was in the process of obtaining my permanent residency in the U.S. We'd had a casual, platonic dinner with the promises of hanging out more, but I soon left the country for the summer, and so, the plans never materialized.

Fast forward another year. As luck would have it, I ran into Juan while having coffee with my friend, Colleen. When he saw me, he came right over and gave me a bear hug, and we immediately started chatting. Colleen was flabbergasted that I'd known this appealing guy for so long, and had never mentioned him to her.

I explained that there had really been nothing to tell. He had become a teacher, and of course, his schedule had not freed him up to come and speak to my classes any longer, although I had, on this occasion, attempted to bribe him to take a day off. While he'd declined the invitation, he did turn around and invite me to have dinner with him to catch up. I could almost hear the soundtrack to Jaws playing in the background. For a good girl like me, Juan was a little dangerous. If anything would happen between us, and I got attached, I knew it was a guarantee that I would be the one to limp away wounded.

But like a child being told not to poke my finger into an electrical outlet, I went ahead and met him for dinner at Applebee's one night after school. This was the first time we had been out for dinner alone, and I was trying to treat it like two buddies who were getting caught up, and not like it was a date. For all I knew, that was exactly Juan's mindset.

When he walked in, still dressed up from work, I was glad to see him. We hugged and sat down. It was strange that he had invited me for dinner, and then proceeded to inform me that he would not be ordering any food! Apparently there had been a school potluck and he was still full. So it seemed that I would be the only one eating. Nothing was coming between an Oriental Chicken Salad and me, so I took the green light and ordered. And for the record, I enjoyed every bite.

Both of us were tired from a long day of teaching, and the conversation started to go off in a peculiar direction. I had never pegged Juan to be a deep thinker, but as it turned out, he didn't only think, but he also thought about what he was thinking, why he was thinking it, and then would analyze why he was thinking about his thinking! (In the field of education, the buzz word for this is metacognition) Did I lose you? I was bowled over that this seemingly easy going man was actually super-analytical. Being relatively free-spirited myself, the amount of reflection I was witnessing right in front of me was overwhelming. Don't get me wrong, I enjoy a deep conversation like anyone else, but Juan was questioning the purpose of life and the intentions of humanity, just to name a few of the "unsolvable" topics.

At this point, I was desperately trying to catch the eye of the waitress in order to start drinking something stronger than an iced tea. If you knew me, you would be surprised by this statement. I rarely drink alcohol. However, the only way I was going to make it through this conversation was going to be with the help of my friend Marg. As in Mango Margarita. She was all I had now, the only relief from the philosophical onslaught that I'd found myself facing. I remember staring at that handsome face only half listening to what he said. "Not fair," I thought to myself. I thought this was going to be a relaxing, fun evening, and instead Juan was only confirming what I'd suspected but was trying to deny - that we have very little in common as far as beliefs and world views.

As I munched on my chicken salad, Juan downed a few more drinks. We had met around 7pm, and by about 9pm the tone of the conversation changed so quickly that I'd almost suffered from mental whiplash. Suddenly we were discussing past dating experiences, and he was teasing me about being a "goody two shoes". He admitted that he'd had one night stands before, which I know is not exactly uncommon for men his age (early thirties). When he'd asked me about my relationship MO, I'd explained to him that I had always been a "serious relationship" girl. He began to tease, saying that the most risqué move I had probably ever made with a guy was to rub sunscreen on his back. He wasn't trying to be a jerk and make me feel bad, but it felt like he was almost daring me to get in touch with my "bad girl" side, so *he* could benefit. I just laughed at him, told him I was proud of my moral compass, and had no intention of being goaded into tossing my values to the wayside on a whim.

Staring into my eyes he inquired whether or not I would be interested in "going back to his place" to watch a movie with him. Translation: I want to get busy with you in the privacy of my own home, and am using the excuse that we will watch a movie to get you there. Juan was really good-looking, and part of me was very tempted to accept his invitation. The other part (the brain part), knew I would feel regret if I became physically intimate with him, only to never hear from him again! Being that we were out on a week night, I told him that it would be better just to hang out at the restaurant and head home afterward. Minor pouting ensued.

Then, I offered up that we should just call it an evening, and this was also deemed unacceptable. That was when he told me that he'd wanted to drink a Brutus, Applebee's largest beer, and that he had not planned to drink alone. It didn't take a rocket scientist to see that he wanted to lower my inhibitions by having me join him. Little did he know that there was NO WAY that I was going to put myself in a precarious position! Another hour and a half went by, and I finally told him I needed to head home, so I would not die the next day when I was expected to teach/entertain a mob of seventh graders!

He insisted that he walk me out to my car. (Oh what, now he had suddenly turned into a gentleman?) When I reached the door he made no immediate move to leave. Being the smooth operator that he was, he somehow ended up in my car with me for a chat. I think he mentioned something about it being cold. Oh wait. It was May in El Paso! It was no doubt over 70 degrees outside.

Before I'd even had a chance to comment, he had pulled me in close to him for a kiss. I'm not going to lie; he was an extremely skilled kisser. Must've been all the practice he'd had during his career as a player! To this day, I can still vividly remember this moment, and I have kissed my fair share of men. To be honest, we seemed to connect better when we weren't talking.

The whole night I had suspected that Juan had an alternate agenda. That is not saying that I thought he was a bad guy. I liked him. But I am going to be honest and confess that I'd really wanted to kiss him too, and had often wondered what that would've been like during our time as students at UTEP. So while he thought he would be "talking me" into a heavy make-out session, what I'd mapped out and maneuvered, was a much more morally acceptable option. The result was a little bit of kissing in the car, after which I headed home relatively unscathed.

I did hear from Juan again once, via text. He'd wanted to confirm that even though we kissed, it was not going to be weird between us. Honestly, we had never really run into each other at the places I frequent, so I was unsure why he was even concerned. Less than a month later I was already talking to Fernando, with the intention to meet him in Seattle. A man with real relationship potential, or a seasoned player? It was no competition.

Back full circle, and 7 months later, (the Fernando relationship officially over) I heard from Juan again. It was strange, but he had unexpectedly passed through my mind briefly a few days before the text. After a few small talk openers, he texted me a simple statement, "I want to see you again." Eyes wide in disbelief, I let him know that this could be arranged. There is a commonly used quote which states that the definition of insanity is to do the same thing over and over again, and to expect different results. Why was I even entertaining Juan's advances? The obvious, blaring reason was his age. He was 32 years old, and had at least 6 years over the oldest of my most recent boy toys. Was it so wrong that I wanted to hop on the dating wagon with someone closer to my age? Someone who had actually heard of Boy George?

Due to the days off we were getting for "STORM 2011", I'd invited Juan to come over to watch movies, (the ones ironically donated by Ben, the now depressed 24 year old). We had already been notified that all El Paso schools would be shut down, so the day after the Super Bowl was a day off! Why not spend it with a beautiful man, in my cozy apartment, on a cold winter's night? When he found my place, I gave him a warm hug and invited him in. Instead of just plopping down on the loveseat, he started circling the living room. Did he not want to sit beside me? Finally he asked,

"Can I sit down?"

"Of course you can! Sorry the love seat is so tiny," I apologized. The first thing that I noticed was how great he smelled. A woodsy scent, with a hint of musk. Juan stayed firmly planted on his side of the loveseat, and I was starting to wonder if he was still attracted to me. Did he like bigger women, and now that I'd lost some weight he wasn't into my look? Did blondes really have more fun, and Juan was more into that type, not feeling my new, significantly darker hair color? Because he had mentioned in one of his texts that on our last visit he hadn't expected to kiss me, but that he also didn't regret it, I was puzzled at the lack of effort to have any physical contact with me.

The first movie started and ended. Nothing. The second movie was well past the half way point. Nothing. It was getting late, and I guessed Juan saw us more as friends, and didn't want to cross that platonic line.

"It's better this way," I silently consoled myself. A relationship with two such opposite types of people could not be successful. Right about this time, Juan grabbed me and pulled me close, wrapping his arm around my shoulder and holding my hand. I had a flashback that only a week before, it had been Ben on the same couch. When the credits started rolling, Juan looked down at me and murmured something. I turned to look up at him, and that is when he started kissing me. Did I mention his cologne made him almost irresistible?

I am obviously not a girl who canoodles with guys casually, and I had no plans on having anything happen but some innocent "making out". At one point, I could tell that Juan was getting riled up, as the intensity of the kissing had suddenly skyrocketed. To my surprise, he decided that it was time for him to leave. I did not have to tell him to slow down, or to stop groping me. A lot of guys claiming to be Christians do not show that kind of restraint, and I was definitely impressed.

To my surprise, there was a text from Juan waiting for me when I woke up the next morning, which stated that he was cold, and he wished I would get into bed with him. A little suggestive, but not astonishing, knowing the type of guy he was. The nagging doubt that he would likely not call or hang out with me again because he knew I was a good girl who would not hook up with him lingered. I managed to push those thoughts away, as I went to meet up with a good friend for some shopping and coffee. Throughout the days that followed, Juan continued to text and ask me how I was doing. I was shocked that not a day went by where I didn't hear from him. After Ben had gone missing in action, it was comforting that another guy was consistently and attentively pursuing me.

The weekend approached, and Juan was trying to pin me down for a time we could get together. By get together, it appeared he meant to cozy up, interlocked on a couch, watching movies. Thus far there had been no suggestions to go to the movie theater, have dinner, or play tennis. I did invite him to come to a karaoke night with my friends, but he'd had his own get together with a friend who had just gotten back from Iraq.

By the end of the week he'd begun texting me and asking when he was going to get another kiss. I had decided to call him out, and via text, asked him what he'd really wanted with me. "Movie buddy," was his reply. I knew it! I let him know that this was an ok classification for us, but that as soon as I started to date someone, I would no longer be watching any movies with him. At this point Juan claimed he had honestly wanted more than just a movie buddy. Hopeful, we did end out hanging out again.

I went over to his house, we spent time together, and I walked out feeling like I knew him better. I also walked out with a little whisker burn. He had asked me what I liked in a man, and when I presented the general traits: intelligent, funny, faith in God, kind, affectionate, and passionate, his immediate response was that I had just described him. We agreed at that time that it might actually be nice to genuinely get to know each other.

Meeting up with him the Sunday before Valentine's Day was risky. I had taken all necessary precautions to ensure that this day, that is only associated with love and crushes, would not take me down without a fight. There would be no renting romantic comedies (such as <u>PS.I Love You</u>), with a full-stocked box of chocolates beside me. There would also be no playing of sad love songs that reminded me of relationships past, which could tragically haunt me like Dickens's ghosts. And there would definitely be no photo albums close by that could lead to tear drop reminiscing over those seemingly ideal men who had come and gone.

All single women know that this holiday is a marketing ploy so that any of us on our own feel lonely. Inherently, we want to feel desirable and loved. As you already know, I am not one to casually cuddle. This is clearly an aspect of me that I also know, but in the case of Juan, I had been trying to make an exception. Even though all that had ever occurred between us was some harmless kissing and snuggling, I somehow still managed to feel more attached than I planned.

To magnify my singleness, I was working at a middle school, which is a central hub of Valentine's Day spirit. At my school, the parents actually purchased and sent their kids huge balloon bouquets, teddy bears, and flower arrangements. All of the young men had given their current "girlfriends" little tokens of their love and affection. Every one of those helium balloons and stuffed animals reminded me that I would likely receive no trinket from a suitor. The best I'd gotten were some chocolate covered strawberries from one of my students, and that doesn't count. (Although it was thoughtful)

I wondered if Juan would at least text and inquire how my day had been? Would he not wish me a Happy Valentine's Day because he was worried it might have seemed that he'd wanted to commit? I did not hear a peep from him all day and night. The military man, Ken, who doesn't speak much, did ask me out for the next day, claiming that he wanted to see me again (You'll meet him next). I suggested a movie, since he was clearly not a chatty guy. Juan, however, had completely dropped the ball.

This had been the test to see if I could actually handle casually dating a man who was obviously attracted to my looks, but not necessarily interested in developing a real relationship with me. Could I handle the fact that a man may have viewed me only as a diversion? In many ways, this was new territory. Guys had usually wanted to be exclusive with me right away. They typically demanded that I not see other people right from the get-go. It had always been this type of a relational pattern over the years. I recognized that I needed to remember that not everyone was looking for an immediate long term relationship. The funny thing was that I'd used to make fun of the girls who had seemed over analytical, and now I could recognize that I was actually one of them!

If, under interrogation, I would've needed to admit that I did not see Juan as a long term partner based on the fact we did not share important beliefs, I would have caved quickly. Did I enjoy his company? Absolutely. He was like a shiny, smooth rock that you'd want to touch and admire, but you wouldn't be fascinated with forever. A novelty.

Now we still text occasionally, and I am not sure if we will ever meet up and hang out as we had planned, however, I am glad I picked up that rock. It was dazzling and entertaining for a time. Hopefully he felt the same way.

- - - - - - - - - - ;*)

Ken: The Silent Wonder

> **I remember contemplating that the date was an hour that I was never going to get back. Such a short, yet excruciating, experience.**

Ken was one of those military transplants who has been mentioned earlier. He'd had two photos on his profile, where it appeared that he was attractive, although not my usual type. Blonde, with green eyes. I usually don't even turn around and give men with these features a second glance, but after emailing and texting briefly, we decided to meet up on a Saturday afternoon. Usually coffee is my go-to date, but since Ken hadn't eaten that day, we'd agreed to meet at Fuddruckers. Since almost everything on their menu is not well-suited for a woman trying to reach her elusive goal weight, I let him order his meal before requesting my usual coffee.

The first surprise of the afternoon was that he did not offer to pay for my plain, non-gourmet coffee. Hadn't he invited me out? Shrugging it off, I pulled out my wallet, grabbed my coffee, and headed for the Splenda. So far, I had not sensed any personal interest from Ken. Not any sparkle in his eye as he spoke. In fact, there had not been a whole lot of speaking going on at all. I can pretty much hold a conversation with anyone. It is not difficult for me to think of topics or questions that keep a steady dialogue going. I'm usually like a wild fire raging through the desert when it comes to conversation. For me, it is usually effortless to find common ground with anyone I meet. Even if a guy ends up being my polar opposite, I can usually encourage him to share details about himself. Right from the start I could see that chatting with Ken was going to be an epic challenge. Every time I would ask him something, I would get a one word response.

Now you are probably wondering why I hadn't asked him questions requiring more than a yes or no answer. Let me clear this up - I did! My reward was to hear crickets chirping. Not a good indication that Ken was interested in getting to know me. I truthfully don't remember being asked one question. The fire was rapidly dying out. It had gotten to the point where I'd literally run out of things to say, which was an all time first for me. If you'd known some of the dates I had been on, you'd realize how dramatic this revelation really was. Sixty minutes in, and I'd finally smiled at him and told him I had forgotten what I was going to ask him (not true - this was the exact moment when I'd had nothing else to say).

Walking out of the restaurant, I had already decided that I would just state that it had been nice to meet him, and then continue on with my day. I remember contemplating that the date was an hour that I was never going to get back. Such a short, yet excruciating, experience.

Sinking into my couch, I'd started watching one of my Net flicks DVDs, attempting to chill out. It was still hard not to feel an iota of rejection. Maybe I just wasn't his type, or he'd found my voice irritating, who knew?

Forty five minutes later, I heard my phone chirp, and discovered that Ken had texted me. The message was simple, but puzzling, "What did you think?" Was this man serious? I'd never thought I'd even hear from this cyber prospect again.

Out of curiosity, I'd responded by asking what he'd meant. "About me ☺," was his immediate reply. That happy face was the most emotional and enthusiastic reaction I had received from Ken thus far, which was why I couldn't even believe that he was contacting me. When he'd followed up with a text declaring, "I want to see you again", I started looking for the TV cameras and Ashton Kutcher.

Was I losing my ability to read whether men were interested in me or not? Up until recently, I'd had almost a flawless record. The question for me was whether I should still attempt to go on date number two with Ken. Maybe he had just been shy because we were meeting for the first time. Maybe he was naturally a quiet guy. After speaking to friends, I was convinced that it was only right for me to give him another chance.

So, the following Saturday we made a tentative plan to go and see a movie. That was my idea, thinking an activity not focused on chatting might be better than wondering if Ken would ever give me more than a three word answer to any of my questions!

As it turned out, he cancelled on me less than an hour before we were scheduled to meet. Frankly, one of my pet peeves is when a guy asks me out, and then changes his plans with me at the last minute. Usually a date does take up the majority of my focus for the day. If I'm really looking forward to it, other errands, priorities, and possibilities are often passed over and ignored. Let me be clear in stating that it is not common for me to accept dates, unless I suspect that it might go somewhere. When I do finally decide to go out with someone, it means that I have recognized some sort of future relationship potential.

After Ken had left me a message to let me know he couldn't make it, without a proper explanation, I'd sent him some irritated text messages. It is amazing how despite the fact you may not be physically speaking to the guy; he can hear the tone of your message. My tone was obviously annoyed and put out. Sensing that he was losing me, he called right away. When I mentioned that I had cancelled plans with friends for the day (which was true), he informed me that the reason he had not been able to meet me was that he was driving a soldier, whose father had died unexpectedly, to the airport. Feeling like one of those high maintenance, unreasonable women, I acknowledged that shame of having so quickly jumped to the wrong conclusion. Or had I? Ken had mentioned getting together an hour after our original time, and when I texted him at 6:30, he let me know he was obligated to fill out some paper work for one of his subordinate soldiers, so he could be reimbursed money from the Red Cross. Now I appeared to be the one who didn't have much to say - who had become the silent wonder. Did Ken want to see me or not? Even though he had reassured me that he couldn't wait to schedule our next date, I wasn't sure that I believed him. Read ahead to find out how things with Ken turned out.

.... ;-)

Feast or Famine: the Invasion Of Fickle Fellows

In short I was carefully watching them play their hands, and calling each how I saw it. "Cheat!" These men played their cards close to their chest, and often have poker faces; yet there is always a giveaway of some kind...

I don't know if it was my sassy new hair cut, or my recent weight loss, but something has awakened within me! Suddenly I felt the impulse to call "CHEAT" on several guys with whom I had been communicating regularly online. Perhaps you have played the card game "Cheat" (the one with the more controversial name of "Bull s@*#"). Once the cards have been dealt, the way to win is to try to convince your fellow players that you are putting down the specific numbers you claim to have in your hand. Cards are always placed on the table face down, so their identities are a mystery. In "Cheat", when you suspect someone is trying to bluff, lie, or trick you in some way, you call him or her out on it, and consequently he or she is forced to pick up whatever cards have been laid down. No one wants to pick up cards, since the whole point is to get rid of your hand.

All at once, the realization had hit me that getting to know some of these online gentlemen had more than a slight resemblance to playing a heated game of "Cheat". Let me explain.

I discovered that I was continuously speaking with multiple men at once, because all of them appealed to me for various reasons. Several of them would lavish attention on me, yet there were red flags that were being raised with each one of them. Commonly, I ignore these warnings, at least in the beginning, and this is exactly what takes place in the card game Cheat.

When you first start playing the game, you don't know anything about your opponent's hand because so few cards have been laid on the table. But as the game continues, you begin to see that your opponent would not likely be laying down 3 kings (because you have 2 of them in your own hand).

In the beginning, most players will wait before confronting their adversaries. In the same way, when online dating, a lack of asking these men the tough questions will prevent any types of disagreements from rearing their ugly heads. I really would try to avoid confrontations because they typically makes both parties feel uncomfortable. Also, I hate to hurt anyone's feelings.

Denial is a powerful tool for the optimistic woman who has taken the online dating world by storm. Knowing that to change a man is a near impossible feat, it is obviously easier to try to ignore the idiosyncrasies we suspect could morph into real problems in the future. In recent days, I had been carefully watching how guys played their hands, and calling them how I saw them. "Cheat!" I'd noticed that these men frequently played their cards close to their chests, only revealing their poker faces. Yet there was always a giveaway of some kind. For some reason, my insight had grown keener. I began picking up on cues that had normally escaped me. Apparently, now I was calling a spade a spade. My incredibly wise sister-in-law coined it, "living my truth".

As a result, those men have scurried away like cockroaches when the lights are turned on. While some would consider my less than subtle tactics juvenile or even self sabotaging, I have to say that I feel that I am conserving my valuable time and energy. Just like in the card game, men don't like to be called out on the carpet. They don't want to admit to anything underhanded, nor do they want to have to "pick up their cards" and accept responsibility for what they may have been dealt, and how they have "played" you.

For example there was Ken, the silent wonder, who'd practically demanded to come over to my house at 11pm on a school night just to "hang out". I'd hardly known this guy, yet he'd wanted to keep me up when I was sick enough to stay home from work? He wasn't offering to pick up medicine, or bring soup. His reason for this erratic request was that he was lonely. LONELY? Then why didn't you call me at 6 pm? (All of the friends with whom I shared this story, had interrupted me at this point declaring, "Booty call!") When I'd asked Ken what he thought we were going to do at 11:30pm (the estimated time of arrival if I had let him come), he replied that we could talk and hang out.

At this point I felt barely human; I was more of a mucus factory. A mountain of Kleenex lay beside me, and my patience was wearing thin. So I called it…."Cheat!" Via text, I made it crystal clear to him that since we hardly knew one another, it was more than a little inappropriate for him to be inviting himself over to my house so late, especially under the circumstances. Sure enough, when I had blatantly shed light on the situation, he'd darted away. His hand was a dud, and Ken was a sore loser!

Another man who turned out to be a game "player" was Hector, my Puerto Rican interest, who had lived on the East side of El Paso. He'd said he was a Christian, so I saw him as having real relationship potential. Also, it appeared that he was a kind person and had a wide range of interests. He'd started texting me every day and even calling me at least every other day.

I liked him. After the first week of communicating, I kept waiting for him to attempt to make plans with me. There was some talk, but nothing materialized. The second week I was fairly sick, so I was not in any real condition to meet him. By the third week, I was sure that since we did live in the same city, we would be able to coordinate a time to get together.

Despite all the "shown" interest via marathon texts and peppy phone calls, he had yet to ask me out. How much preamble is really necessary for a coffee date? When I'd mentioned that I had started packing for my upcoming week-long trip, he still made no concentrated effort to attempt to meet in person before I was due to leave. Something about that made me call, "Cheat!" I told him that I did not believe he was very interested in me or we would have already gone out on a date.

At this announcement, Hector had been highly offended. In fact, he'd even said I was mean. When I'd replied that I was just being honest, he'd told me I was making assumptions. Answering that accusation, I calmly texted that it was no goal of mine to have to guess about his intentions, and I'd only wanted to see where he stood. The straw that broke the camel's back was when I'd pushed the envelope and told him the right girl for him was still out there. He told me I was shoving him away, and that he "got" what I was doing. I did try to smooth things over, but he wasn't having any of it. I'd just wanted him to say something like, "I really do like you, and the reason we haven't met yet is because….." or, "Why don't we just drop what we are doing and get together for coffee in 20 minutes?"

Maybe the truth was what I had already guessed when I called "Cheat" that he was unsure about his interest in me. Or maybe I intuitively sensed that he had a terrible hand, and he resented that. I wondered if he was even who he'd said he was. Maybe he was angry that I'd caught him with a bad hand. I have no regrets about how I played the game, as these relationships were not meant to be.

Unfortunately, the most disappointing thing about playing "Cheat" with your online suitors is that when you have to call them out, everyone loses. They bolt, and you are left to pick up the cards.

Reaching For the Brass Ring?!

MY ARDUOUS ONLINE DATING EXPERIENCE could be compared to an action-packed and long awaited 12 hour excursion to Six Flags.

How long had it taken me to reach my destination? A week? A month? Years? My entire life? Like any amusement park - I would need to shell out some coin to get in and be able to take advantage of all that was offered. This was a small price to pay for the fun I knew I was going to have. I have felt eagerness similar to this when I first discovered online dating sites. There were hundreds, no thousands of men, who were all waiting to meet me! I could only imagine the entertaining and enjoyable dates on which I was sure to be invited.

The die-hards buy season passes so they can enter the park at will, whenever the urge hits them. When perusing match making sites, the ones that have the potential for the best guys (I won't literally compare men to rides here), are going to cost you to join. The creators of these venues will offer their version of a seasons pass, but they call them "holiday specials". Did you know that for less than a dollar a day, you might meet your soul mate? Who could resist that pitch?

When first embarking on the quest to discover love in cyberspace, it is similar to when you first walk into a theme park. Strolling through the gates, the smells, sounds and sights playfully tease your senses. Loud, throbbing music helps create the party atmosphere. The sounds of laughter and squeals are like a melody to your ears! Colored lights blink and flash everywhere.

There are all sorts of foods that are always accessible at an amusement park. For those that love sweets, they can indulge in devouring funnel cakes, cotton candy, mini donuts, and ice-cream. Others who prefer more salty delights can choose to munch on buttery popcorn, pretzels, chips, or hot Cheetos. There is a match for every palate. In cyberspace I have encountered men from all walks of life. Some were the "bad boys" and advertised that fact without shame. Others portrayed themselves as sweet and sensitive, and appeared to be the perfect boyfriends. There were the homebodies and the party animals. Existing side by side were the couch potatoes and the marathon runners. A match for every palate, indeed. Did I just compare men to food?

Once good money has been paid to get into a pricey amusement park, many people will devise a game plan for how to tackle the feat of being able to get on the best rides, avoid the longest lines, and take in as many of the activities as possible. You can attack the park in one of two ways. There is the organized and calculated route, or you can choose to just wing it, and go wherever you want, whenever you want.

I feel that was my attitude has always been very deliberate when I joined a site. The first tasks to undertake were always completing some advanced searches and specifying what criteria were my "deal breakers". Some sites even have filters, and this helped to sift through some of the creeps who are married or had other issues that I had no desire to deal with. Occasionally, to mix things up, I would just browse through different profiles of men who were online or even out of town. You never know where the treasure may be buried! These are the types of strategies that will help you get the most out of your online dating website membership. (For more tips, see Chapter 4)

Sometimes the rides, attractions and live shows that you expected to be a main source of entertainment for you, will either be temporarily closed down or out of order. The disappointment that you may feel can overshadow your enjoyment of being at the park, tempting you to just head home and cut your losses.

There are times that I have joined a venue that promised handsome Christian men to meet, and then it would appear that many of them were "out of commission" (their memberships had expired) or lived so far away that bridging the distance seemed impossible. Closed until further notice. My encouragement to you is that new members join these websites every day. Check back later to see if the attractions are playing or open. Perhaps a great possible match will suddenly appear!

Once a plan has been set in motion to try to gleam the most out of the amusement park experience, you can be ready to experience unbelievable thrills! It's easy to get caught up in all the hype and energy, moving from ride to ride. Some spin, some drop, some twist and turn. Some do it all backwards. Some of the tracks contain hairpin turns. You determine your own level of "risk."

Everyone who has joined the online dating community has different "thrill" levels. In amusement parks the different themed areas are all distinct and interesting, just like online dating. Some people I know have gone to all the trouble to set up a profile, and then don't even muster up the nerve to meet anyone. Others will meet anyone at anytime. Those are the people who ride in the very front of those rickety old wooden roller coasters, with their arms up in the air, and their eyes wide open. I fit somewhere in the middle, a calculated risk taker.

Sometimes those risks will pay off, and you will meet someone with great potential. An example of this would be one of the best first online dates I'd ever had with Josh. Though he had no picture on his profile, I took a chance and met up with him. When we were connecting, and the sparks were flying between us, it felt like the split second before approaching the summit of a mighty roller coaster. It was exciting, but a little daunting, with my stomach tied in knots. Of course, what goes up must come down—often at high speed. A lot of online connections seem to pack a punch and are exhilarating for an instant, but like the ride eventually ends, often, so does the relationship.

A lot of amusement parks have special "flash" tickets that customers can buy in order to bypass the long and tiresome lines for the most popular rides. That is how many cyber daters are hoping that their search for love will be - they just want to side-step having to go out on awkward dates, and would rather find their match immediately. The owners of these websites will cater to this desire, and you can buy access to features where your profile is highlighted, where you can know the exact moment he/she has opened your email, etc. I hate to be the one to break it to you, but unless you are the "lottery winning type", you have to be willing to endure some uncomfortable circumstances to reach your goal, flashy features or no flashy features. I did have a great friend who met her husband almost immediately after she had joined an online dating site. After having spent years on the cyber space love circuit, I wanted to both strangle and high five her at the same time! For most of us, it is going to be a numbers game.

The grand finale at a superior park is to be able to last until the fireworks show takes place at the end of the night. I have heard it is spectacular, but the only way I will know for sure is to last the whole day, in order to see it for myself. We all want that romantic relationship with the grand lights and sound display that is being promised like a carrot to a bunch of eager Easter bunnies.

But there is a problem.

The amusement parks always appear shiny and new at first, but eventually, you start to notice all the different sections and areas that are run down and in shabby condition. The wooden decks and stairs might even be splintered and rotten in the heavy traffic areas. Will I make it until almost closing time to see the big show? Can I ever find that person with whom I'll inexplicably feel that chemistry, and with whom there is real relationship potential? The excitement of being in the park wanes while waiting in line for hours, wondering if your turn to experience the ride will eventually materialize. When you have scoured the sites, and are just not running into any more prospective dates, it feels like it will take forever to encounter someone who might actually be a match. Your patience is tested.

The temptation is to just leave the line and give up the opportunity to ride. Also there comes a point, especially when you live in an area lacking in a singles scene, that you will begin constantly viewing the same people on the dating sites. This could be compared to the point at which all the rides start to feel the same. After several hours, the desire to be part of the adventure begins to fade. The loud music starts to irritate, and even causes the beginnings of a headache. People-watching becomes people-avoiding, as the crowds start to get on your nerves. The food which smelled irresistible at first, starts to make you feel nauseous, especially as you realize how outrageously expensive it is.

At times dating online can be downright scary. You get that nervous pit in your stomach when you don't feel "safe", whether physically or emotionally. On my dicey date with Justin, where I thought he would leave me for dead in the desert, I felt that my life was possibly in jeopardy. In my relationship with

Fernando, at the end - during the last twists and turns of that ride, I felt my emotional well being was in jeopardy, and had to leave, cutting my losses.

Even through all the ups and downs, bumps and jolts of my journey, I have realized that seeking love online did not tear my identity down, but if anything, I believe that it has made me stronger and more self-aware. This trek has definitely helped me to laugh at myself, and not take things as personally as I used to. It is easy to see a dismissal as being a personal rejection. However, I have found that you should recognize that an individual preference does not indicate that a person isn't good enough for you, or that you are not good enough for the other person. As a result, I have become a more self-accepting woman. Now I don't assume that I look too fat, too old, or that something else is wrong with me if there is no chemistry present. After all, if a guy leans towards being attracted to redheads with curly hair, I shouldn't feel dejected if he is not attracted to me. We all have our fondness for different traits: broad shoulders, a clean cut look, a scruffy beard, a certain height, a particular eye color, or a million other traits. As stated earlier, I have never been one to do a double take when a blond man passes me on the street, but that is just my personal liking, and I have learned that everyone else has the right to their own preferences.

I have also learned to be tenacious in searching for that soul mate. Despite my growing cynicism, I am still a hopeless romantic who believes that the right man is still out there. I persist in searching online for him, as my everyday life is not conducive to meeting single men.

Accepting others as they are, even if that means that they are not meant to be in a romantic relationship with me, is another discovery I have made. Everybody has value and worth, but it is a rare event when two people have enough in common to create a real connection. I am still friends with several men I have met online, and consider them to be valuable people in my life, although we were not meant to be romantically involved.

While I may feel that cyber love eludes me, much like the illusion that I could ever win while playing one of those deceptive carnival games, the hope is that one day that monstrous, pink stuffed animal will be mine!

It is my belief than one night I will be found sitting on a grassy slope, enjoying that festive firework display, hopefully cuddled up to the one I love. Until then, I celebrate that after a long hard day at the park, I am able to return home.

Made in the USA
Charleston, SC
24 September 2011